Historic Highways of America

Volume 6: Boone's Wilderness Road

ARCHER BUTLER HULBERT

Historic Highways of America 6
Jazzybee Verlag Jürgen Beck
86450 Altenmünster, Loschberg 9
Deutschland

ISBN: 9783849674892

www.jazzybee-verlag.de
admin@jazzybee-verlag.de

Printed by Createspace, North Charleston, SC, USA

CONTENTS:

PREFACE

THE naming of our highways is an interesting study. Like roads the world over they are usually known by two names — the destinations to which they lead. The famous highway through New York state is known as the Genesee Road in the eastern half of the state and as the Albany Road in the western portion. In a number of cities through which it passes — Utica, Syracuse, etc. — it is Genesee Street. This path in the olden time was the great road to the famed Genesee country. The old Forbes Road across Pennsylvania soon lost its earliest name; but it is preserved at its termination, for the Pittsburger of today goes to the Carnegie Library on the " Forbes Street" car line. The Maysville Pike — as unknown today as it was of national prominence three quarters of a century ago — leading across Ohio from Wheeling to Maysville (Limestone) and on to Lexington, is known in Kentucky as the Zanesville Pike; from that city in Ohio the road branched off from the old National Road. The "Glade Road" was the important branch of the Pennsylvania or Pittsburg Road which led through the Glades of the Alleghenies to the Youghiogheny. One of the most singular names for a road was that of the " Shun Pike " between Watertown and Erie, in northwestern Pennsylvania. The large traffic over the old " French Road " — Marin's Portage Road — between these points on Lake Erie and French Creek necessitated, early in the nineteenth century, a good road-bed. Accordingly a road company took hold of the route and improved it — placing toll gates on it for recompensation. Those who refused to pay toll broke open a parallel route nearby, which was as free as it was rough. It became known as the " Shun" Pike because those who traversed it shunned the toll road. Few roads named from their builders, such as Braddock, Forbes, Bouquet, Wayne, Ebenezer Zane, Marin, and Boone preserved the old-time name. Indeed nearly all our roads have lost the ancient name, a fact that should be sincerely mourned. The Black Swamp has been drained, therefore there can be now no " Black Swamp Road." There are now no refugees and the " Refugees Road" is lost not only to sight but to the memory of most. Perhaps there is but one road in the central West which is commonly known and called by the old Indian name; this is the " Tuscarawas Path," a modern highway in Eastern Ohio which was widened and made a white man's road by the first white army that ever crossed the Ohio River into what is now the State of Ohio.

One roadway — the Wilderness Road to Kentucky from Virginia and Tennessee, the longest, blackest, hardest road of pioneer days in America — holds the old-time name with undiminished loyalty and is true today to every gloomy description and vile epithet that was ever written or spoken of it. It was broken open for white man's use by Daniel Boone from the Watauga settlement on the Holston River, Tennessee, to the mouth of Otter Creek on the Kentucky River in the month preceding the outbreak of open revolution at Lexington and Concord. It was known as " Boone's Trail," the " Kentucky

Road," the " road to Caintuck," or the "Virginia Road," but its common name was the " Wilderness Road." A wilderness of laurel thickets lay between the Kentucky settlements and Cumberland Gap and was the most desolate country imaginable. The name was transferred to the road that passed through it. It seems right that the brave frontiersman who opened this route to white men should be remembered by this act; and for a title to this volume " Boone's Wilderness Road " has been selected.

As in the case of other highways with which this series of monographs is dealing, so with Boone's Wilderness Road: the road itself is of little consequence. The following pages treat of phases of the story of the West suggested by Boone's Road — the first social movement into the lower Ohio Valley, Henderson's Transylvania Company, the struggle of the Watauga settlement to prevent the southern Indians from cutting Kentucky off from the world, the struggle of the Kentucky settlements against the British and their Indian allies, the burst of population over Boone's Road into Kentucky, and what the early founding of that commonwealth meant to the East and to the West.

Boone and Harrod and their compatriots assured the world of the splendid lands of Kentucky; Richard Henderson and his associates of the Transylvania Company proved the questionable fact that a settlement there could be made and be maintained. Boone's Road, opened for the Transylvania Company, made a way thither. The result was a marvelous westward movement that for timeliness, heroism and ultimate success is without a parallel in our annals. When the armies of the Revolutionary War are counted, that first army of twenty-five thousand men, women, and children which hurried over Boone's little path, through dark Powell's Valley, over the "high-swung gateway" of Cumberland Gap, and down through the laurel wildernesses to Crab Orchard, Danville, Lexington, and Louisville must not be forgotten. No army ever meant so much to the West; some did not mean more to the East.

The author is greatly indebted for facts and figures to Thomas Speed's invaluable study The Wilderness Road, and to other Filson Club Publications, and for inspiration and suggestion to Mr. Allen's The Blue Grass Region of Kentucky.

A. B. H.
Marietta, Ohio, May 20, 1903.

CHAPTER I - THE PILGRIMS OF THE WEST

NO English colony in America looked upon the central West with such jealous eye as Virginia. The beautiful valley of the Oyo — the Indian exclamation for " Beautiful " — which ran southwesterly through the great forests of the continent's interior was early claimed as the sole possession of the Virginians. The other colonies were hemmed in by prescribed boundary lines, definitely outlined in their royal charters. New York was bounded by Lake Erie and the Allegheny and thought little of the West. The Pennsylvanian colony was definitely bounded by the line which is the western boundary line of that commonwealth today. Carolina's extremity stopped at thirty-six degrees and thirty minutes. Virginia's western boundary was not defined; hence the West was hers.

England herself was not at all sure of the West until after the fall of Quebec; but the Treaty of Paris was soon signed and, so far as the French were concerned, the colonies extended to the Mississippi. Then Pontiac's bloody war broke out and matters were at a standstill until Bouquet hewed his way into " the heart of the enemies' country" and, on the Muskingum, brought Pontiac's desperate allies, the Delawares and Shawanese, to terms.

But now, when the West was his, the king of England did a wondrous thing. He issued a proclamation in the year 1763 which forbade anyone securing " patents for any lands beyond the heads or sources of any of the rivers which fall into the Atlantic Ocean from the West or Northwest! " Thus Lord Hillsborough, British Secretary for the Colonies, thought to checkmate what he called the " roving disposition " of the colonists, particularly the Virginians. The other colonies were restrained by definite boundaries; Virginia, too, should be restrained.

Hillsborough might as well have adopted the plan of the ignoramus who, when methods for keeping the Indians from crossing the frontier were being discussed, suggested that a strip of land along the entire western frontier be cleared of trees and bushes, in the belief that the savages would not dare to cross the open! Yet the secretary's agent set to work to mark out a western boundary line which should connect the western lines of Georgia and New York and so accomplish the limitation of Virginia.

But the Virginians also acted. They sent an agent of their own, Thomas Walker, to Fort Stanwix (Rome, New York) to treat with the Six Nations for some of this very western land that Hillsborough was contriving to keep them out of. For the king issued the proclamation in the interest of the western Indians (and the annuities he received when the fur trade was prosperous) who desired that the West should be preserved to them. But what could be said if Virginia purchased the Indian's claim? Could a king's proclamation keep the Virginians from a territory to which, for value received, the Indians had given a quit-claim deed?

3

This famous Treaty of Fort Stanwix was held in the fall of 1768. Three thousand Indians were present. Presents were lavished upon the chieftains. The western boundary line crossed from the west branch of the Susquehanna to Kittanning on the Allegheny River; it followed the Allegheny and Ohio Rivers southwest to the mouth of the Great Kanawha. Here it met Hillsborough's line which came up from Florida and which made the Great Kanawha the western boundary of Virginia. Had the Fort Stanwix line stopped here the western boundary line of the colonies would have been as Lord Hillsborough desired. But Walker did not pause here. Sir William Johnson, British Indian Agent for the Northern District, who was " thoroughly versed in the methods of making profit by his office, " allowed Walker to extend the line so as to enclose Virginia's prospective purchase; and the Tennessee River was made the western boundary instead of the Great Kanawha. Thus Johnson at once satisfied the claims of Virginia and the pride of the Six Nations, who were still anxious to prove their long-boasted possession over the Cumberland region, as well as their sovereignty over the hated Cherokee, by thus formally disposing of the land. So everyone was satisfied — but Hillsborough. And yet the Crown was compelled, finally, to approve the Treaty of Fort Stanwix.

This treaty marks an epoch in the history of the central West, since, thereby, nearly half of it became a portion 'of one of the Thirteen Colonies. The other half, north of the Ohio River, remained in the possession of the Indians who inhabited it.

It is remarkable how little known that great territory was which now became a part of Virginia. This was largely because it was an uninhabited country. The territory north of the Ohio River was filled with Indian nations, some of whom had reigned there from times prehistoric. This was likewise true of the country south, where the great southern confederacies had held sway since white men came to this continent. But between these inhabited areas lay a pleasant land which any tribe would have gladly possessed had there not been so many rivals for it. Consequently it became a " dark and bloody " land where a thousand unrecorded battles were fought by Indians from both North and South who had the temerity to come there to hunt, or by armies who were hurrying through it in search of their foes who lived beyond. No Bouquet had pierced through to the Cumberland to release prisoners who might bring back reports of the land. No missionaries had carried their " great and good " words to this battle ground of the Nations and returned with tidings of its splendid meadows and their fertility. One or two adventuresome explorers had looked there and brought back practically all that the world knew of it. But they had never visited the most pleasant portions and knew little, if anything, of its real value. And all the Indians seemed to know was that it was a bloody border-land where no tribe could hunt in peace; where every shadow contained a lurking foe; and where every inch of soil was drenched with blood.

Thus to an unknown and unoccupied border-land between the Indians of the North and those to the South, Virginia obtained, from one of its alleged possessors, a nominal hold. Could she maintain it? The world asked the question and awaited the answer, wonderingly.

The principal reason why Virginia was successful was because her inhabitants were an agricultural people like their ancestors before them in England. Being an agricultural people they had expanded further, geographically, than the inhabitants of any of the other colonies. As early as 1740, cabins were being built in Bedford County, Virginia, over one hundred and fifty miles from the seaboard. There were settlements on the New River, a branch of the Great Kanawha, before the French and Indian war. Fort Loudoun, over the border, was erected in 1756, and Forts Long Island and Chissel in 1758. The Wyoming massacre in New York State in the Revolutionary War occurred on what was then the frontier, though Wyoming was less than a hundred miles from New York City. And, fortunately, this agricultural people was located in the most favorable place along the Atlantic for expansion, for a reason already mentioned. Back of New York and Pennsylvania roamed the Iroquois, Delawares, Shawanese, and other Indian nations. Back of Virginia, whose fine rivers rose in the mountains, lay a comparatively uninhabited country; for, the moment the Indians became allied with either of the encroaching European powers, they ceased contending together in the border-land behind Virginia. It was not until Virginians began to occupy it that it became anew a " dark and bloody ground." Virginia knew less of Indian warfare than some of the neighboring colonies until the era of her expansion when her sturdy people began occupying the land obtained at the Treaty of Fort Stanwix.

The expansion of Virginia was greatly facilitated by the geographical position of the mountains along her western frontier. While the mountains of western New York and Pennsylvania obstructed expansion, in Virginia the mountain ranges facilitated it. Further north they trended directly north and south and even the rivers could find a passage-way only by following the most tortuous courses. True, the Hudson and Mohawk valleys offered a clear course to the great highland across to the Niagara River, but it was not until very late in the eighteenth century that the path across this watershed was open to white men. The two routes through Pennsylvania crossed the mountains horizontally and almost feared to follow the waterways. Braddock's Road crossed the waters of one stream three times at right angles in the space of eighty miles and did not follow it one hundred yards altogether. In Virginia the mountain ranges trend southwesterly, with the rivers between them, offering a practicable though roundabout route westward.

But there was another thing Virginia possessed in addition to an agricultural people — an uninhabited territory west of her and some plain courses into it. She had among her citizens some daring, farsighted, energetic men who might easily be called the first promoters of America. They were moneyed men who sought honestly to make money; but they were also men of chivalry and intense patriotism — Virginians of Virginians. They thought of their pockets, but they also thought of their colony and their king; the standing of the Old Dominion was very dear to them: its growth in commercial as well as geographical dimensions. They desired to be thought well of at home; they desired that Virginia should be thought the best of all America.

Of these men the Washingtons were the most prominent, and George Washington was a marvelously inspired leader. As early as 1749 Virginians secured a grant of land south of the Ohio and directly west of old Virginia. The enterprise amounted to nothing save by precipitating the contest between England and France for the West. The example of the younger Washington in fighting for the possession of the West, in encouraging the disheartened people of the frontier in the dark days of defeat, in aiding in the final victory, in investing heavily in western land (for he, it is said, died the richest man in America, and half his wealth lay west of the Alleghenies), in encouraging the building of the Potomac Canal, in impressing upon the people the commercial value of exploiting the entire West from Lake Huron to Cumberland Gap, affords perhaps the most remarkable instance in our whole national history of one man inspiring a people to greater things. A place and a rough way thither was ready for expanding Virginia — and such sons as Washington gave the inspiration.

Through the great " trough " between the Allegheny and Blue Ridge ranges passes the pioneer route to which we of the central West owe as much as to any thoroughfare in America — that rough, long, roundabout road which, coming down from Lancaster and Yorktown, crossed the Potomac at Wadkin's Ferry, and passed up the Shenandoah valley by Martinsburg, Winchester and Staunton; and on to the headwaters of the New River, where it was joined by the thoroughfare through central Virginia from Richmond. Here, near the meeting of these famous old-time Virginia thoroughfares, stood Fort Chissel, erected in 1758 and situated two hundred miles east of Cumberland Gap. Beyond Fort Chissel ran the Indian trail toward the Gap and, within fifty miles of the Gap, stood Fort Watauga on a branch of the Holston.

This was the most westerly fort at the time of the Stanwix treaty, and about the rude fort was springing up the Watauga settlement. Other earlier settlements were made at Draper's Meadows and at Inglis Ferry on New River by families bearing those names. For more than a century the population of Virginia and North Carolina had been slowly sifting up the river valleys toward the West and by the time the king's proclamation was issued many cabins were already erected beyond the headwaters of streams which fell " into the Atlantic Ocean from the West or Northwest. " Even the faithful Hillsborough seems to have recognized this since his boundary line passed through Chiswell's Mine on the Great Kanawha and the mouth of that river — much further west than a strict interpretation of the proclamation would allow.

This vanguard which was moving westward was led by explorers and hunters. Of two of the former, mention will be particularly made. The parties of hunters who now began to press beyond the furthest settlements, while they subsisted on game, were also real explorers of the West and helped to set in motion and give zest to the great immigration which followed the signing of the Stanwix treaty. It was only one year after the Stanwix treaty when Daniel Boone came up from his home on the Yadkin in North Carolina and led a company of men through the Gap into the land whose hero and idol he was ever to be. About the same time John Finley and party were trapping on the forbidden rivers, and Colonel James Knox and company of nine hunted on the New, Clinch, and Holston Rivers, and reaching even to the lower Cumberland in 1769-70. These parties of men found that a paradise for the husbandman was to be speedily revealed to the world at the foothills of the Cumberland and Pine mountains on the great plain falling away westward to the Mississippi. At first, only the most vague description of the rich meadows of the West reached the Virginian settlements, but, meager as they were, they started a tide of immigration quite unparalleled in American history. One of these descriptions is preserved for us in the autobiography of Daniel Boone, and, though couched in language with which he was probably less familiar than his amanuensis, still is not unlike the stories told in border cabins to eager listening frontiersmen who were soon on their rough way to this El Dorado beyond the horrid ranges of the Cumberlands:

" We found everywhere abundance of wild beasts of all sorts, through this vast forest. The buffalo were more frequent than I have seen cattle in the settlements, browsing on the leaves of the cane, or cropping the herbage on those extensive plains, fearless, because ignorant of the violence of man. . . Nature was here a series of wonders and a fund of delight. Here she displayed her ingenuity and industry in a variety of flowers and fruits, beautifully colored, elegantly shaped and charmingly flavored; and we were diverted with innumerable animals presenting themselves perpetually to our view. . . Just at the close of day the gentle gales retired and left the place to the disposal of a profound calm. Not a breeze shook the most tremulous leaf. I had gained the summit of a commanding ridge, and, looking around with astonishing delight, beheld the ample plains, the beauteous tracts below: On the other hand had I surveyed the famous Ohio river, that rolled in silent dignity, marking the western boundary of Kentucky with inconceivable grandeur. At

7

a vast distance I beheld the mountains lift their venerable brows, and penetrate the clouds. " Inspired by such descriptions as these, there came in the wake of the hunter-explorers crowds of immigrants. Very many came even bringing their families, for the novelty of the adventure and because there was nothing to keep them where they had had but a tomahawk claim on the border. There were thousands who entered the West and became valuable citizens (considering the work to be done) who would best be described as gypsies. For a larger part of the way across the continent this peculiar class of people moved westward between the advanced explorers and the swarm of genuine " settlers " whose feet, even at this time, were making the middle of our continent tremble. For instance, very many of the first settlers in the territory near the Mississippi hailed from a portion of the land between their home there and the Allegheny mountains, just as many of the first settlers between the Ohio and Lake Erie hailed from Virginia's land between the Ohio and Tennessee. The phrase " following the immigration " was a common one and covered this class of pioneers who moved away from a given district of land when it began to fill with settlers. There has appeared a disposition in some quarters to attempt to minimize the value of the hosts of so-called " squatters" and " tomahawk claimers " who first moved into the West. Our pioneer literature is full of discreditable allusions, made by the second tide of pioneers who came West, concerning the scattered ranks of first comers, their moral character, their ways of thought and living. The later blueblood stock had not a little to say concerning the pioneers of Western Virginia and Kentucky flavored with the same spice that Dickens employed when, a little later, he jotted down his " American Notes." It seems as though it were reasonable to remember what these first comers did rather than the picture of what they were. But for them there could never have been a better West. Who composed the armies of Mcintosh, Brodhead, Crawford, Harmar, St. Clair, and Wayne but these rough, wild-looking men who first entered the West? What is now western Pennsylvania, West Virginia, and Kentucky gave practically all the troops which conquered the land between the Ohio River and the Great Lakes. And all of them, save the few who could raise money to buy some of it, retired again to their slovenly " claims " south of the Ohio — and a flood-tide of newcomers came after them to bring a new era they could never have brought, and, incidentally, leave to posterity repulsive pictures of them. It hath been said: " Instead of the thorn shall come up the fir tree, and instead of the brier shall come up the myrtle tree; and it shall be to the Lord for a name, for an everlasting sign that shall not be cut off. " The West was a land of brier and thorn, and men as rough as briers and thorns were needed to strike the first swift hard blows. The squatter in the West played an important part and should not be remembered solely by the pictures drawn of his filth, lawlessness, and laziness. The Cleaveland of 1798, was a paradise beside the Cleveland of 1810. Was it not Caleb Atwater who said that " not one young man, whose family was rich, and of very high standing in the Eastern States, has succeeded in Ohio?" A little later in this narrative we shall read of one " Abraham hanks " who went, an unknown pioneer, with Daniel Boone through Cumberland Gap at the very van of all the western immigration! Atwater was not referring to his grandson — the immortal son of Nancy Hanks. Theodore Roosevelt in the following words has emphasized the debt our country owes to this class of early citizens: " Nevertheless this very ferocity was not only inevitable, but it was in a certain sense proper; or at least, even if many of its manifestations were blamable, the spirit that lay behind them was right. The backwoodsmen were no sentimentalists; they were grim, hard, matter-of-fact men, engaged all their lives long in an unending struggle with hostile forces, both human and natural; men who in this struggle had acquired many unamiable qualities, but who had learned likewise to appreciate at their full value the inestimable virtues of courage and common-sense. The crisis [Revolution] demanded that they should be both strong and good; but, above all things, it demanded that they should be strong. Weakness would have ruined them. It was needful that justice should stand before mercy; and they could no longer have held their homes, had they not put down their foes, of every kind with an iron hand."

With these uncouth border families moved another class of men known as land speculators. The schemes of these fortune hunters and of the many great companies of which they were the representatives would fill a moderate volume and can only be hinted at here. As we have noted, a company was organized very early to speculate in western lands, called the Ohio Company. It received from the king of England a grant of land between the Monongahela and Great Kanawha Rivers, but failed to fulfil the required conditions and the Charter reverted to the Crown. From that day to the breaking out of the Revolutionary War numerous land companies secured by one means or another a claim to certain lands and many sought such claims but never secured them. It will be necessary to refer to one of these companies later in the course of our narrative.

Near the front in this race for the rich meadows between the Ohio and Tennessee were bounty-land claimants. One of Virginia's most effective pleas for the great territory which had come into her possession was that she might reward her soldiers of the French and Indian wars. While as a people she had known less of Indian warfare than some of the colonies, Virginia had been liberal in sending troops northward to defend the frontier. And these Virginians had made a name for themselves at Braddock's defeat and elsewhere. Washington was always insistent that the claims of these old veterans of the bloody border war be redeemed in good lands, and it must be remembered ever with pride that as late as 1770, only six years before he became commander-in-chief of the armies of the United States at Cambridge, and but two years after the signing of the Stanwix treaty, he made the difficult journey to the Ohio River and down that river in a canoe to Virginia's new empire on the Great Kanawha, where surveys of bounty lands for his heroes of Fort Necessity were first made. Additional surveys were soon made along the Ohio and Licking Rivers. Explorers, hunters, squatters, speculators, and bounty-land claimants — this was the heterogeneous population that was surging westward to the land of which Boone wrote. But not all came down the old thoroughfare between the Allegheny and Blue Ridge Mountains and through Cumberland Gap. Many followed northward the rough trails which descended the New and Monongahela Rivers, while many went northwesterly over Braddock's overgrown twelve-foot road or along the winding narrow track of Forbes's Road through the Pennsylvania Glades to the little frontier fortress, Fort Pitt. From the time Bouquet relieved this beleaguered garrison until the Stanwix treaty, Pittsburg, as the town was now known, had been growing. One year after that treaty (1769) the manor of Pittsburg was surveyed, the survey embracing five thousand seven hundred and sixty-six acres. Upon the signing of the Stanwix treaty, Pittsburg became an important point and was claimed by both Pennsylvania and Virginia. About it sprang up villages and from it down the Ohio and up the Allegheny and Monongahela Rivers settlements spread. What was loosely known as the " Monongahela Country " — the territory between the Monongahela and Ohio Rivers — became quite populous.

Here, high up along the Ohio River, the Virginians learned how to fight the red man, if they had never known before. The decade succeeding Pontiac's war, though nominally a peaceful one, was, nevertheless, one long and bitter duel between the Indians north of the Ohio and the Virginians who were coming " in shoals" to its southern bank. It has been estimated that the total loss of life within that decade was as great as the total loss in the open war — Dunmore's War — which soon broke out and which momentarily threatened the extinction of Virginia's great colonial movement into the southern half of this black forest of the West.

We have refrained from using the name Kentucky long enough, perhaps, to accomplish the purpose of impressing upon the reader's mind the part Virginia and the Virginians played in the creation of the earliest settlement in the West, first known as the county, then the state, of Kentucky. As Professor Shaler has said: " She owes to Virginia the most of the people she received during the half century when her society was taking shape: her institutions, be they good or evil, her ideals of life, her place in the nation's history, are all as immediately derived from her great Mother Virginia as are an individual man's from the mother who bore him."

The name Kentucky, Kentuckgin, Kantucky, Kentucke, Caintuck, as it was variously spelled, may have been derived from an Iroquois word Ken-ta-kee, which means " among the meadows. " When, in the olden days, only the long, painted canoes of the Iroquois could be moored in safety in the shades of the woodland meadows south of the Oyo, the name Ken-ta-kee was first heard — a name which has come down to us so pregnant with pride and power. The Catawba River, which gained its name, perhaps, from the famous war-path which followed it toward the land of the Catawbas in the south, was first known as the Louisa River (named by Walker in honor of the wife of the " Bloody Duke" of Cumberland), and afterwards as the Kentucky River.

After the treaty at the close of Dunmore's War, Virginia had two quit-claim deeds to her western empire: one from the Iroquois, who boasted their possession of it, and one from the Shawanese, who had disputed the settlement. There was yet another claimant to deal with, the Cherokees of the South. In the year following the battle of Point Pleasant (1774) a land company headed by Colonel Richard Henderson purchased from the Cherokees the land between the Ohio, Kentucky, and Cumberland Rivers. This purchase was achieved at Fort Watauga through the agency of Daniel Boone. This private purchase from the Indians was afterward annulled by both Virginia and North Carolina, but so far as the Indian claims to Kentucky were concerned it had passed into the possession of the white man. Every inch of soil had been fairly obtained from each and every claimant who had made it a " dark and bloody ground " through their battles for it, since the earliest period of recorded history. But at the time of the Cherokee purchase, an old Indian chief said to Boone: " Brother, we have given you a fine land, but I believe you will have much trouble in settling it." Perhaps the Cherokees knew what Shawanese quit-claim deeds were worth! After making this purchase for Colonel Henderson, Boone engaged to mark out a road through Cumberland Gap to the center of the newly acquired territory. Following the old trail through the Gap, Boone's Road ended at a new settlement at the mouth of Otter Creek on the Kentucky River named Boonesborough, in his honor. Fort Boonesborough was completed July 14, 1775. Colonel Logan and party came westward through the Gap at the same time but diverged from Boone's Road on Rockcastle Creek, and opened the more important branch of the road toward Louisville by way of Crab Orchard and Danville, and erected Fort Logan one mile west of Standford, in what is now Lincoln County, Kentucky. Harrod's, Logan's, and Boone's forts were the important early " stations " in the West. To them the thousands wended their tedious way over the " Wilderness Road," as both branches (Logan's and Boone's) were fitly called, or down the Ohio from Pittsburg. And along these lines of western movement cabins and clearings made their rapid appearance despite the era of bloodshed which began almost simultaneously with the opening of the Revolutionary War in the East.

Such were the pilgrims of the West. It is interesting to note that these leaders of civilization in the West were true Americans — American born and American bred. It is remarkable that the discoverers of the American central West were either French or American. For the work of exploring this hinterland, England scarcely furnished a man; she can write no names opposite those of Brulé, Cartier, Champlain, Du Lhuth, Hennepin, Joliet, Marquette, and La Salle. Nearly all that England knew of the interior she learned from the French. Her great explorers were maritime explorers and her conquest of New France was effected by water. But while the West could not have for its first colonists the counterpart of the hardy, irresistible race who first came to the Atlantic seaboard, it did have the next best thing — the direct descendants of them. It was a race of Americanized Britons who pressed from Virginia into the West. Hardly a name among them but was pure Norman or Saxon. Of the twenty-five members of the Political Club at Danville, Kentucky, which discussed with ability the Federal Constitution, all but two were descendants of colonists from Great Britain and Ireland. Of forty-five members of the convention which framed Kentucky's first constitution, only three could claim European ancestry. Of the seven hundred members of the Filson Club, the representative historical society of Kentucky today, there are not more than twenty who are not either English, Scotch, Welsh, or Irish. The blood of the mother country flowed in purer strain in no portion of the continent at the outbreak of the Revolutionary War than in the Virginian settlement of Kentucky. That the blood was true to its fighting traditions is proved by the Revolutionary pension rolls. In 1840 there were nine hundred Revolutionary soldiers receiving pensions in Kentucky. This race gave to the West its real heroes — the Gists, Walkers, Boones, Clarks, Todds, Shelbys, Kentons, Logans, Lewises, Crawfords, Gibsons, and St. Clairs. In frontier cabins they were bred to a free life in a free land — worthy successors to Washington and his school, worthy men to subdue and rule the empire of which they began the conquest before the outbreak of the Revolutionary War. In the form of these sturdy colonizers the American republic stretched its arm across the Appalachian mountain system and took in its grasp the richest river valley in the world at the end of Boone's Wilderness Road. That arm was never withdrawn, that grasp never relinquished. The leaven of old Virginia leavened the whole lump.

Thus may be outlined briefly the era of expansion in which Boone's Road played an all-important part. In the succeeding chapters the phases of this historic movement are reviewed as the meager data now obtainable can permit.

CHAPTER II - THE FIRST EXPLORERS

THE first real explorations of the great territory secured by Virginia at the Treaty of Fort Stanwix were made by Dr. Thomas Walker, who later so skillfully managed Virginia's part of that treaty, and Christopher Gist, in the early years of the second half of the eighteenth century, 1750 and 1751.

The brief journals written by these men are the sources of our first information concerning the vast territory west of the Appalachian mountain system — the eastern half of the Mississippi basin south of the Ohio River. They are meager records of hard day's pilgrimages, an outline of the routes pursued, and a description of the lands which were traversed. Both were explorers for two newly formed land companies. Walker represented the Loyal Land Company of London, and Gist was the representative of the Ohio Company. The company for which Walker acted had secured a grant of eight hundred thousand acres in the territory now embraced in Kentucky north of 36 30'. The Ohio Company had a grant of five hundred thousand acres between the Kanawha and Monongahela Rivers. These men were sent to search out favorable lands and report on the giants and grapes. They found both.

Little suggestion of the romance and daring of these historic journeys can be found in either of the journals of them; they make slight books. But volumes can be written on what can be read by the most careless reader between their few lines. The long climbing over the almost pathless mountains, the nights spent in discomfort, the countless trials, fears, dangers of which they knew so much and told so little — all this should make a story if it never has, that could not by any means find an uninterested reader. No youth's history is of moment until we know the man and know that he is a man among men. Our nation is still a boy. Only with the passing of the years will its boyhood be studied and known as it should be known; when that time comes, the brief stories of such men as Walker and Gist will appear of priceless value.

" Having, on the 12th of December last, been employed for a certain consideration to go to the Westward in order to discover a proper Place for a Settlement, I left my house on the Sixth day of March, at 10 o'clock, 1749-50, in Company with Ambrose Powell, William Tomlinson, Colby Chew, Henry Lawless & John Hughs. Each man had a Horse and we had two to carry the Baggage. I lodged this night at Col. Joshua Fry's, in Albemarle, which County includes the Chief of the head Branches of James River on the East side of the Blue Ridge." Thus begins Dr. Walker's journal. At this time England and her colonies were dating by the old calendar, each new year beginning on the twenty-fifth of March. Accordingly they started nineteen days before the beginning of the year 1750.

It was a brave little company of adventurous men. Walker had attended William and Mary College, and then had joined the ranks of that distinguished army of representative Virginians who, with saddle-bags and surveying instruments, proved to be the vanguard of the army which was to achieve the real conquest of the West. His home was Castle Hill, near Charlottesville, Albemarle County, Virginia, where his companions had rendezvoused for the present expedition and from which point they began their historic journey. Powell was of the best Virginian stock, and has left his name to one of the great valleys through which the highway to the West ran. His son became a Revolutionary officer and his great-grandson was General A. P. Hill, the famous Confederate leader. Chew was from Orange County, Virginia, and belonged to the Maryland branch of the Chew family. Two Presidents of the United States, Madison and Taylor, could claim him as a relative. Seven years later he served in Washington's regiment in Forbes 's expedition against Fort Duquesne, and was killed in Grant's wild attack on that fort. As the journal states, this company spent the first night out with Colonel Joshua Fry. Fry too was one of them in spirit, though he did not accompany them westward. He was a graduate of Oxford University, joint author with Jefferson of Fry and Jefferson's celebrated Map of Virginia, and a commissioner for the crown in establishing the boundary line between North Carolina and Virginia. He was killed by being thrown from his horse while taking command of Washington's expedition against Fort Duquesne, four years later. These statistics show plainly that the best brain and blood of Virginia was foremost in attempting to realize Virginia's dream of conquest and expansion. But it was a time for brave men to show themselves. Ambitious Virginia had been slow to claim the West, where even at this early date Frenchmen had gone so far into the wilderness. Celoron, bold emissary of the humpbacked Canadian Governor Gallissoniere, was now burying leaden plates at the mouths of the rivers which emptied into the Ohio, as a sign of French possession of the West. One of these was placed at the mouth of the Great Kanawha " at the mouth of the river Chinodahihetha, this 18th day of August," claiming for the Bourbon crown the entire territory in which the grant of land to the Ohio Company was located. There was not a moment to lose if the West was to be saved to England. A settlement must be made quickly, and Walker and his band pushed on immediately to find a " proper Place for a Settlement."

But all this, seemingly, is neither here nor there — so far as Walker's Journal is concerned. There is not one mention of the political crisis then at hand; instead of French claims, Walker deals with tired horses or broken-legged dogs, and where one might suppose he would mention national boundary lines he tells only of cutting names on trees. And at the end, where the reader might look for a summary statement of the results of his tour he finds this: " I got home about noon. We killed in the Journey 13 Buffaloes, 8 Elks, 53 Bears, 20 Deer, 4 Wild Geese, about 150 Turkeys, besides small game. We might have killed three times as much meat, if we had wanted it." Yet, so far as human interest is concerned, the record is exceptionally entertaining, and to a student of the great thoroughfare from Virginia to Kentucky it is full of meaning; because of its many references to the difficulties of traveling at that early date, and to the varied experiences of explorers on the earliest thoroughfares westward. It is this story of experience in traveling west in 1750 that makes Walker's Journal of interest in the present study.

On the day after the party left Colonel Fry's, "We set off about 8," writes Dr. Walker, " but the day proving wet, we only went to Thomas Joplin's on Rockfish. This is a pretty River, which might at a small expense be made fit for transporting Tobacco; but it has lately been stopped by a Mill Dam near the Mouth to the prejudice of the upper inhabitants who would at their own expense clear and make it navigable, were they permitted." Virginia's great industry evidently flourished this far from tidewater even at this early date, though handicapped by these dams which were erected by the " Averice of Millers, " on which Dr. Walker comments again in his next day's record. The record for Sunday, the eleventh, is appropriately brief: " 11th. The Sabbath." In only one or two instances did the party travel on Sunday, and then the journey was occasioned by necessity. On the twelfth the party crossed the Upper James River above the mouth of the Rivanna, and lodged with one Thomas Hunt.

" 13th. We went early to William Calloway's and supplied ourselves with Rum, Thread, and other necessaries & from thence took the main Waggon Road leading to Wood's or the New River. It is not well clear'd or beaten yet, but will be a very good one with proper management." Wood's River — or New River, as we know it today — was discovered in 1671 by Colonel Abraham Wood, who explored along the line which later became the boundary line between North Carolina and Virginia. He crossed the Alleghenies through " Wood's Gap" (now Flower Gap) and, going down Little River, found New River not far from Inglis Ferry, where Walker's party crossed three days later. This mention of the road Walker traversed is his first reference to the great road westward toward Cumberland Gap; he remarks its roughness, but before he returned to Virginia he learned new lessons on rough roads. " This night we lodged in Adam Beards low grounds. Beard is an ignorant, impudent, brutish fellow, and would have taken us up, had it not been for a reason, easily suggested." When thus brought in contrast with the hospitality usually tendered Walker's party, the deportment of this churlish mountaineer is conspicuous. Travelers on these first highways were ever in need — if for nothing more than a camping-place. The people who settled beside the frontier roads were trained by bitter experience to a generous hospitality. This hospitality was particularly marked, throughout the colonies, among those who could afford it, especially on the frontiers; and here it was often bestowed upon travelers when it could be ill-afforded. The modern hotel has in a large measure relieved the general public from the burden of

15

continual and promiscuous hospitality, and it has been found that where hotels are least known this prime requisite of an expanding civilization may still be found. On the frontier, men were dependent on those who lived beside the road, not only in time of accident and sickness, but at all times — for little food and forage could be carried. At times travelers nearly perished when once beyond the frontier line. Walker's party, though they killed the large amount of game mentioned, were once compelled to kill and eat one of their dogs. Captain Estill, who lost his life in Kentucky in the engagement which bears his name, is said to have done a great service for emigrants from Virginia by killing game and leaving the meat beside the road, in order to " pass on and notify incoming trains where they might find a supply of meat."

Instances of vile treatment of travelers are not often cited, but the few that exist are the exceptions that prove the rule of generosity which was common to the time.

Leaving Beard's, Walker and his men went, on the fourteenth, to Nicholas Welch's, " where," the Doctor writes, " we bought corn for our horses, and had some Victuals dress'd for Breakfast." From here they climbed the Blue Ridge through Buford's Gap, in Bedford County, through which the Norfolk and Western Railroad now passes. " The Ascent and Descent is so easie," writes Walker, " that a Stranger would not know when he crossed the Ridge." On the day after, they reached " the great Lick" near the present city of Roanoke, and continued up the trail on the following day to near the historic Inglis Ferry, not far from the present village of Blacksburg, Montgomery County, Virginia. From this on, Walker's route is not of importance to our study, as he missed the great trail which would have taken him to the pleasant meadows of Kentucky — though he struck it again at Cumberland Gap but did not follow it — and wandered over a circuitous route thus outlined by Daniel Bryan: " They started from low down in Virginia, traveled westwardly across Alleghany Mountains to Chissel's Lead Mine, on New River; thence into the Holston Valley, thence over Walden's Ridge and Powell's Mountain into Powell's Valley. . . They then continued down the valley, leaving Cumberland Mountain a small distance on their right hand, until they came to Cumberland Gap. . . At the foot of this mountain they fell into an Indian path leading from the Cherokee towns on Tennessee River to the Shawnee Indian towns on the Ohio, which path they followed down Yellow Creek to the old ford of Cumberland River. . . Thence they went on the path down the river to the Flat Lick, eight miles; here they left the river, continued on the path, turning more north, crossing some of the head branches of the Kentucky River over a poor and hilly country, until they concluded there was no good country in the West. They then took an easterly course over the worst mountains and laurel thickets in the world. . . They crossed the Laurel or Cumberland Mountain and fell into the Greenbrier country, almost starved to death .. and reached home with life only to pay for all their trouble and suffering."

Regretting that this opinion of the final value of Walker's journey cannot be gainsaid, it is yet of interest to follow his footsteps and learn what were some of the experiences of such early explorers as these.

On the twenty-sixth they " left the Inhabitans," as Dr. Walker called the line of civilization, and were at last within the wild land where no settlers had yet come. On the night of the twenty-ninth the " Dogs were very uneasie," and the next day, on Reedy Creek, a branch of the South Fork of the Holston, the tracks of a party of Indians were discovered, which explained the restlessness of the dogs. It is probably little realized in this day how valuable dogs were to explorers and immigrants. They were not only of service in giving warning of the approach of strangers, but were well-nigh indispensable in securing game and in searching for lost horses. Dr. Walker's love for dogs is a tradition in the family, and his care of them on this journey is typical of the gentleman and the wise frontiersman. At the junction of Reedy Creek and the Holston — an historic spot in Tennessee — Walker found a gigantic elm tree, which measured twenty-five feet in circumference at a distance of three feet from the ground. Pioneers and explorers considered the study of trees a fine art. By this means they always judged the quality of the soil, and knew at a glance by the growth that stood on it the character of any piece of land. The diaries of all that old school of western adventurers contain frequent mention of trees which were an almost infallible criterion of the soil beneath. Washington had keen eyes for trees — as for everything else — as illustrated in the journal of his trip down the Ohio River in 1770. On the fourth of November he found a sycamore on the Great Kanawha, in comparison with which this first elm of Walker's was insignificant. It measured, three feet from the ground, forty-five feet in circumference, and nearby stood another measuring thirty-one feet around. Upon hearing about this larger tree, someone remarked that Washington might have told the truth about the cherry tree but he told a " whopper " about the sycamore. But it was not guess-work, for the record states clearly that the girth of the larger tree lacked two inches of being the complete forty-five feet. Trees along the Ohio grew to an immense size; an old Ohio River pilot affirms that in his boyhood a burned trunk of a sycamore stood on his father's farm on the Little Muskingum, into which he has frequently driven a horse, turned it about, and come out again. General Harmar found on the Ohio a buttonwood tree forty-two feet in circumference, which held forty men within its trunk. On the seventh of April Dr. Walker writes: "It snowed most of the day. In the evening our dogs caught a large He Bear, which before we could come up to shoot him had wounded a dog of mine, so that he could not Travel, and we carried him on Horseback, till he recovered." On the thirteenth the party reached " Cave Gap," which Walker named Cumberland Gap in honor of the

" bloody Duke," the hero of Culloden. " Just at the foot of the Hill is a Laurel Thicket. . . On the South side is a plain Indian Road. on the top of the Ridge are Laurel Trees marked with crosses, others Blazed and several Figures on them. . . This Gap may be seen at a considerable distance, and there is no other, that I know of, except one about two miles to the North of it, which does not appear to be So low as the other. The Mountain on the North Side of the Gap is very Steep and Rocky, but on the South side it is not So. We called it Steep Ridge."

The party crossed the Cumberland River about four miles below the present village of Barbourville, Knox County, Kentucky, on the twenty-third of April. The river was named by Walker at this time. From this spot Walker, with two companions chosen by lot — Powell and Chew — went on a tour of exploration alone, leaving the others " to provide and salt some Bear, build an house, and plant some Peach Stones and Corn."

Walker and his two companions floundered about the neighboring region for five days, not getting out of the mountainous country and not finding any good land. They crossed the Cumberland again, on the third day out, about twenty miles below the first crossing-place, and then returned up the river to the main party and found that the work he had ordered to be done was completed. " The People I had left had built an House 12 by 8, clear'd and broke up some ground, & planted Corn, and Peach Stones."

Thus was raised, beside the tumbling Cumberland, on the farm now owned by George M. Faulkner four miles below Barbourville, Kentucky, the first house now recorded as built by white men in the fine territory between the Cumberland Mountains and the Ohio River, now the state of Kentucky. It was not an " improver's cabin " — a log pen without roof — but a roofed house, and instituted what the English Loyal Land Company could claim to be a " settlement " in the territory which they had been granted. This was completed by the planting of corn and peach trees. The formality of this " settlement " is evinced by the fact that, two days later, the entire party moved on for further exploration, never again to return to their house or to reap their crops. It was twenty years before a house was erected in Kentucky for the permanent dwelling.

From this on, Dr. Walker's journal is a long story of accidents and disappointments. One horse became lame, and " another had been bit in the Nose by a Snake."

" I rub'd the wounds with Bear's oil, and gave him a drench of the same and another of the decoction of Rattle Snake root sometime after." On the same day " Colby Chew and his Horse fell down the Bank. I Bled and gave him Volatile drops, & he soon recovered." On the first of May they reached Powell's River. This was named from Ambrose Powell. During the journey Dr. Walker gave the name of each of his companions to rivers he discovered; none were given his name, though a mountain range to the north of Fort

Chiswell still bears the name of Walker's Mountain. On Powell's River the party this day again struck the Indian path which later became the great highway to Kentucky. Again he was on the route that would have taken him to the famous meadows below the foothills of the mountains, and again he left it as he did when he chose to explore on the south side of Cumberland Mountain, instead of crossing at Pineville and following the trail northward. He did not cross Rockcastle River. J. Stoddard Johnson says: " This was the farthest western point reached by Doctor Walker. He did not cross the main Rockcastle River, and, therefore, was never on the waters of Salt or Green rivers, as claimed by some. A day or two's travel to the west or northwest would have brought him to the fertile lands of Lincoln or Madison County, his description of which would have left no doubt of his having passed the watershed between the Rockcastle, the Salt, and the rivers to the westward."

Shoes formed an important item in the catalogue of necessaries for the early traveler's outfit on the first traveled ways in America. Already Walker's party, though they traveled largely by horse, had worn out the shoes with which they started, and on the eleventh of May under one of the great cliffs near Rockcastle River they set to work to make themselves new shoes out of elk-skin. " When our Elk's Skin was prepared," writes Dr. Walker on the fourteenth, " we had lost every Awl that we brought out, and I made one with the Shank of an old Fishing hook, the other People made two of Horse Shoe Nails, and with these we made our Shoes and Moccosons." On the twenty-third the party was on the Kentucky River, where Walker found a sycamore which measured forty feet in circumference — almost, it will be seen, the size of the tree Washington found on the Great Kanawha — upon which he marked his initials, " T. W." On the day after, he found another sycamore thirty feet in circumference. These trees, it would naturally be inferred, marked the location of fertile soil. On the twenty-sixth the " Dogs roused a large Buck Elk, which we followed down to a Creek. He killed Ambrose Powell's Dog in the Chase, and we named the Run Tumbler's Creek, the Dog being of that Name."

" 31st. We crossed 2 Mountains and camped just by a Wolf's Den. They were very impudent and after they had twice been shot at, they kept howling about the Camp. It rained till Noon this day."

" June ye 1st. We found the Wolf's Den and caught 4 of the young ones." It was very common for frontiersmen to invade the dens of wolves without any opposition on the part of the old wolves. Wolf cubs have often been pulled away from their mothers, who would only snarl and show their teeth. Bears, on the other hand, would fight to the death any invader of their dens. Notions which commonly prevail today, about the dangers in the primeval forests of America from wild animals, undergo a great change after a careful reading of pioneer literature.

On the fourth of June " a very black Cloud appearing, we turn'd out our Horses, got tent Poles up, and were just stretching a Tent, when it began to rain and hail, and was succeeded by a violent Wind which Blew down our Tent & a great many Trees about it, several large ones within 30 yds. of the Tent. We all left the place in confusion and ran different ways for shelter. After the Storm was over, we met at the Tent, and found all safe."

On the fourteenth the party had gone east as far as the dividing ridge between the two forks of the Big Sandy; but within a few days the horses were spent, and the whole party floundered onward afoot. On the twentieth they reached Flat-top Mountain, Raleigh County, West Virginia. This day Dr. Walker's horse was bitten by a snake; " . . having no Bear's Oil," he wrote, " I rub'd the place with a piece of fat meat, which had the desired effect."

Passing the present site of Hinton, West Virginia, the party followed about the present line of the Chesapeake and Ohio Railway. They crossed the Allegheny divide July 8, and Hot Springs the ninth. They found " Six Invalides there. The Spring Water is very Clear & warmer than new Milk, and there is a spring of cold Water within 20 feet of the Warm one. I left one of my Company this day." They reached Augusta Court House (Staunton, Virginia) on the eleventh, and Castle Hill on the sixteenth, having been four months and seven days on the journey.

Walker's hard tour amounted to very little for the plain reason that he never got west of the mountains. He found no good land and his report was depressing.

It remained for another brave frontiersman to go further and bring back the welcome news of large areas of splendid land in the Ohio Valley. In 1748 John Hanbury, London merchant; Thomas Lee, President of the Council of Virginia; and a number of prominent Virginians formed the Ohio Company, elsewhere mentioned, and received a large grant of land in the West. The grant was made March 18, 1749: two hundred thousand acres between the Monongahela and Great Kanawha Rivers, and later three hundred thousand acres, to be located on the waters of the lower Ohio. In 1750 this company employed Christopher Gist, a hardy, well-trained frontiersman who lived on the Yadkin in North Carolina, to explore the Ohio Valley and make a report upon the land there found. For his arduous service he was to receive one hundred and fifty pounds sterling " and such further handsome allowance as his service should deserve. " His instructions read as follows: " You are to go out as soon as possible to the Westward of the great Mountains, and carry with you such a Number of Men as You think necessary, in Order to Search out and discover the Lands upon the river Ohio & other adjoining Branches of the Mississippi down as low as the great Falls thereof: You are particularly to observe the Ways & Passes thro all the Mountains you cross, & take an exact Account of the Soil, Quality & Product of the Land, and the Wideness and Deepness of the Rivers, & the several Falls belonging to them, together with the Courses & Bearings of the Rivers & Mountains as near as you conveniently can: You are also to observe what Nations of Indians inhabit there, their Strength and Numbers, who they trade with, & in what Comodities they deal. " When you find a large quantity of good, level Land, such as you think will suit the Company, You are to measure the Breadth of it, in three or four different Places, & take the Courses of the River & Mountains on which it binds in Order to judge the Quantity: You are to fix the Beginning & Bounds in such a Manner that they may be easily found again by your Description; the nearer in the Land lies the better, provided it be good & level, but we had rather go quite down the Mississippi than take mean broken Land. After finding a large Body of good level Land, you are not to stop but proceed further, as low as the Falls of the Ohio, that we may be informed of that Navigation; And You are to take an exact Account of all the large Bodies of good level Land, in the same Manner as above directed that the Company may the better judge when it will be most convenient for them to take their Land.

" You are to note all the Bodies of good Land as you go along, tho there is not a sufficient Quantity for the Company's Grant, but You need not be so particular in the Mensuration of that, as in the larger Bodies of Land.

" You are to draw as good a plan as you can of the Country You pass thro: You are to take an exact and particular Journal of all Your Proceedings, and make a true Report thereof to the Ohio Company."

Gist was the man for the business in hand. He came from an enterprising family and was well educated. His father was one of the Commissioners for laying off the city of Baltimore. " Little is known of his early life, but the evidences he has left in his journals, his maps, plats of surveys, and correspondence indicate that he enjoyed the advantages of an education superior to that of many of his calling in those early days. His signature and manuscript are characterized by the neatness and uniformity of a copy plate, while his plats and surveys are models in their mathematical exactness and precision of drawing. To this evidence of scholarly order and professional skill he added the hardy qualities of the pioneer and backwoodsman, capable of enduring the exposure of long journeys in the most rigorous weather. In him were combined the varied talents which made him at once an accomplished surveyor, an energetic farmer who felled the forest and tilled the soil, a skillful diplomat who understood the Indian character and was influential in making treaties, a brave soldier, an upright man, trusted by the highest civil and military authorities with implicit faith."

The earlier portion of Gist's journey, which he began in October, 1750, is not of importance in the present monograph. He reached the Ohio River by way of the Juniata and. Kiskiminitas Rivers. Crossing the Ohio he worked his way westward on the Great Trail to the " Crossing Place of the Muskingum

" (Bolivar, Ohio), and from thence he traversed the Indian trail to the country of the Shawanese and Miamis.

It was not until Tuesday, the twelfth of March, that Gist again crossed the Ohio, and entered what is now the state of Kentucky. His first day's experience was typical — in a land so well known for great things and strong; for on the day after crossing at the Shawanese Shannoah Town, he found two men who had " Two of the Teeth of a large Beast. . . The Rib Bones of the largest of these Beasts were eleven Feet long, and the Skull Bone six Feet wide, across the Forehead, & the other Bones in Proportion; and that there were several Teeth there, some of which he called Horns, and said they were upwards of five Feet long, and as much as a Man could well carry."

Gist was now in Kentucky — the land of which thousands were waiting to hear, the home of the race that was to come and conquer and settle and hold the West. Of it Gist came to know only a little, but this little was the beginning of a revelation.

After crossing the Ohio, Gist journeyed over a hundred miles down the southern bank of the river, and on March eighteenth crossed " the lower Salt Lick Creek," the Licking River. Reports of Indians at the "Falls" and "the footsteps of some Indians plain on the Ground" made him desist from visiting that spot, but he took down descriptions of it. On the nineteenth he turned southward into the interior. On the twentieth he ascended Pilot Knob, near Clay City, Powell County, and writes of the view from that height from which he saw, as John Finley wrote later, " with pleasure the beautiful level of Kentucky."

With but a glimpse of the good lands of Kentucky, Gist, like Walker before him, journeyed into the mountainous country to the southeast. For a month he floundered around in the desolate laurel ridges where Walker had spent so many distressing days the year before. On Red River Gist crossed Walker's route and came on homeward between Walker's outward and homeward courses. From Red River he went through Pound Gap and eastward, down what is known as Gist's or Guesse's Fork of the Clinch in Wise County, Virginia, and then upon Bluestone, a tributary of New River. On the thirteenth of May he crossed Walker's route again at Inglis Ferry, near Draper's Meadows. On the seventeenth he passed into North Carolina through Flower or Wood's Gap toward his home on the Yadkin. He reached home on the eighteenth and found that his family had removed to Roanoke, thirty-five miles eastward, because of depredations of the Indians during the winter.

Gist's journey was far more successful than Walker's. He found the fine fertile valleys of the Muskingum, Scioto, and Miami Rivers north of the Ohio, and he caught a glimpse of the beautiful meadows of Kentucky. He singularly made a complete circle about the land between the Monongahela and Kanawha Rivers, where the Ohio Company's grant of land was made. As he did not approach it on any side it is probable that he knew that only rough land lay there. Had it not been for the sudden breaking out of the old French War, the Ohio Company would undoubtedly have settled on lands in the Ohio Valley according to Gist's advice. Hostilities on the frontier soon drove back the farther settlements, and rendered activities in the land Gist had discovered out of the question, either on the part of land companies or private individuals.

CHAPTER III - ANNALS OF THE ROAD

WITH the close of Pontiac's Rebellion and the passing away of the war clouds which had hung so long over the West, ten thousand eyes turned longingly across the Alleghenies and Blue Ridge. War with all its horrors had yet brought something of good, for never before had the belief that a splendidly fertile empire lay to the westward taken such a hold upon the people of Virginia. Nothing more was needed but the positive assurance of large areas of good land, and a way to reach it. It was ten years after the close of Pontiac's war before both of these conditions were fulfilled.

First came the definite assurance that the meadows of Kentucky were what Gist and others had reported them to be. The Proclamation of 1763, forbidding western settlement, did not forbid hunting in the West — and the great emigration which started as slow as a glacier was finally put into motion by the proof brought back to North Carolina and Virginia by the hunters (of whom mention has been made) who went over the mountains between 1763 and 1773. In 1766 Colonel James Smith, undaunted by his captivity among the Indians, hunted through the southern portion of Kentucky. In 1767 John Finley traded with the Indians in northern Kentucky, and James Harrod and Michael Stoner were in the southern portion of the country. Finally, in 1769 Daniel Boone came into the land " a second Adam in another Eden." Boone reached the edge of the beautiful Blue Grass Region and returned home in 1771 to tell of what he saw, and to bring his family " as soon as possible to live in Kentucky, which I esteemed a second paradise, at the risk of my life and fortune." In 1769 also, the party of stout hunters headed by Colonel James Knox reached Kentucky, and hunted on the Green and Lower Cumberland Rivers; they were so long absent from home that they were given the name of "The Long Hunters." These, too, brought glowing descriptions of the fine meadows of Ken-ta-kee.

At once the forests were filled with cohorts of surveyors — the vanguard of the host under whose feet the continent was soon to tremble. These surveyors represented the various land companies and the bounty land seekers, who had a claim to the two hundred thousand acres promised the Virginian soldiers in the old French war. Scores of cabins were raised in 1774 at Harrodsburg, near Danville, on the east fork of Salt River, on Dick's River, and on Salt River. Their erection marks the beginning of the first settlement of the land one year previous to the breaking out of the war of the Revolution.

These first comers found their way to Kentucky by two routes — the Warriors' Path through Cumberland Gap, and the Ohio River, which they reached either by the Kittanning Path up the Juniata or by Braddock's or Forbes's Roads. Each route was dangerous and difficult beyond description. It was a terrible road from Cumberland to Pittsburg, and the journey down the Ohio was not more inviting. When the river was high and afforded safe navigation it was as much a highway for red men as for white — and these were treacherous times. When the river was low, a thousand natural obstructions tended to daunt even the bravest boatmen — and the Virginian backwoodsmen were not educated to contend with such a dangerous stream as the Ohio, with its changing currents, treacherous eddies, and thousands of sunken trees. One frontiersman who made the river trip at an early date, cautioned those who essayed the trip against rowing their boats at night; lest the sound of the oars should prevent the watchman from hearing the " riffling " of the water about the rocks and sunken trees, on which many a boat had been wrecked with all its precious freight. The danger of river travel down such a stream appealed with tremendous force to the early pioneers, with the result that the majority chose the land route.

But what an alternative! A narrow trail in the forests six hundred miles in length was the only path. It had been traversed by many even as early as 1775, but each traveler had made it worse, and the story of the hardships of the journey through "the Wilderness" would make even the bravest pause. It is a hard journey today, one which cannot be made without taxing even the strongest; what was it before the route was dotted with cities and hamlets, before the road had been widened and bridged, before the mountains had been graded and the swamps drained, before the fierce lurking enemies had been driven away?

Neither Walker nor Gist traversed what became the famed Wilderness Road to Kentucky. When the Shawanese raided Draper's Meadows, near Inglis Ferry, in 1755, they took their prisoners away on the trail through Powell's Valley toward Cumberland Gap; and the rescuing party which followed them were perhaps the first white men who traveled what became the great pioneer thoroughfare to Kentucky. It was, undoubtedly, the route followed by the early hunters who passed through Cumberland Gap and found the fertile meadows of which Dr. Walker was ignorant, and of which Christopher Gist caught only a faint glimpse. Settlements sprang up slowly beyond Inglis Ferry, but by the time of Boone's return in 1771 a few families were on the upper waters of the Holston, and settlements had been made on the Watauga where Fort Watauga was soon to be built, and at Wolf Hills, now Abington. These settlements were all one hundred miles east of Cumberland Gap, and the little path thither was not yet marked for white man's use.

But the brave Boone was as good as his word — and he did attempt to bring his family and five other families to Kentucky in the year 1773, over what was soon to be known as Boone's Road. This was the beginning of the great tide of immigration through Cumberland Gap, a social movement which for timeliness and ultimate success ranks as the most important in the history of the central West. This initial attempt was not a success, for the party was driven back by Indians, with loss, entirely discouraged. But from this time on, despite Dunmore's War which now broke out, the dream of western immigration could not be forgotten.

But all the western movement was now put at hazard by the outbreak of this cruel, bloody war between the " Long Knives" — as the Virginians in the Monongahela country came to be called, from the sabers that hung at their loins — and the Shawanese north of the Ohio. As suggested, the preceding years had been marked by continual bloodshed. It is undoubtedly true that those Long Knives on the upper Ohio had been doing some dreadful slashing. Perhaps the provocations were as enormous as the crimes; surely the Indians to the north were the most bloodthirsty and cruel of any on the continent. At the same time it is safe to say that many of their white foes on the Ohio were inhuman marauders, whose principal occupation was that of shooting game for a living and Indians for sport. Even in the statement in Boone's autobiography there is a plain suggestion of a guilty conscience on the part of those of whom he wrote: " The settlers [in the Monongahela country], now aware that a general warfare would be commenced by the Indians, immediately sent an express to Williamsburg, the seat of government in Virginia, communicating their apprehensions and soliciting protection." How aware? Because some of the relatives of the Indian chieftain Logan had been basely murdered, while intoxicated, on Yellow Creek?

The Virginian House of Burgesses was quick to answer this appeal of the western colonists, and Governor Dunmore's earnestness in arranging the campaign resulted in the short wars bearing his name. General Andrew Lewis, a hero of Braddock's defeat, was commissioned to raise an army of border settlers and march down the Great Kanawha; while Lord Dunmore went northward to Pittsburg, where, in the Monogahela country, he would recruit another army and descend the Ohio to the mouth of the Great Kanawha. Here the armies would unite to pierce the valley of the Scioto in which the hell-hound Shawanese dwelt.

Lewis gathered an army of eleven hundred experienced borderers from the Watauga settlement and the Greenbriar Valley, and marched swiftly northward. But the enemy knew of his approach, and instead of joining Dunmore's army at the mouth of the Great Kanawha he met a barricaded Indian horde, equal in size to his own army, and the bloody and momentous battle of Point Pleasant was fought and won. Arriving at the Ohio, Lewis encamped on the point of land between the two rivers. Soon two hunters pursuing a deer encountered the Indian vanguard which was bearing down on the ill-placed army of whites. One hunter fell dead and the other returned with the alarming news. General Lewis, a pupil in that school on Braddock's Road, lit his pipe and ordered the assault. Two regiments advanced on the Indian line, which now ranged from river to river, completely cutting it off from retreat. Both colonels commanding were soon killed and their men began to fall back disconcerted. Reinforcements drove the redskins back to their entrenchments, and renewed confidence. But at last fighting became desperate. Among his Virginians, the brave Flemming, twice wounded, kept repeating his order, " Advance, outflank the enemy and get between them and the river." Among his desperate followers the calm voice of Cornstalk was heard all day long: " Be brave, be brave, be brave! " As in the battle of Bushy Run, where the hope of the West lay with Bouquet as it did now with Lewis, so at Point Pleasant no way of success was left, at the close of that October day, save in strategy. The white man did not learn to conquer the red until he learned to deal with him on his own terms of cunning and deceit.

In desperation Lewis sent three companies up the Great Kanawha under cover of the bank to Crooked Creek. Ascending this stream with great caution, these heroes of the day rushed from its bed upon the enemy's flank, and the tide of the battle was turned. The Indians, though having suffered least, fell back across the Ohio to their villages to the northward. The proposed junction of the two white armies was achieved, but Lewis had already sufficiently awed the Shawanese, who came to Dunmore's Camp Charlotte in their valley, and gave their affirmation to the Fort Stanwix Treaty, which surrendered to the whites all the territory south of the Ohio and north of the Tennessee.

In less than a year Boone went through the Gap alone to the " Falls of the Ohio " (Louisville), and returned in safety, more possessed than ever with the ambition to take his family to the El Dorado which he had discovered, and of which he spoke in the enthusiastic vein which has already been quoted. He had found the splendid lands of which Gist had guessed; he had found a straight path thither. All that was lacking was an impetus to turn a floodtide of Virginians and their neighbors into the new land.

This came, too, within a year after the close of Dunmore's War — an artificial impetus in the shape of a land company, headed by a brave, enterprising man, Colonel Richard Henderson, with whom were associated eight other North Carolinians of high social standing. Richard Henderson was the son of Samuel Henderson (1700) and Elizabeth Williams (1714). He was born in Hanover County, Virginia, on the twentieth of April, 1735. His two well-known brothers, Nathaniel and Pleasant, were born in 1736 and 1756, respectively. The sons were worthy of their good Scotch-Welsh ancestry. When Richard was about ten years of age his father moved from their home in Virginia to Granville County in the province of North Carolina. Here the elder Henderson was afterward appointed sheriff of his county, and the young Richard was soon able to assist his father by doing the business " of the sherriffltry. "

After this practical introduction to the science of law young Richard turned to the theoretical study, and read law for a twelve-month with his cousin, Judge Williams. In that day a prospective barrister was compelled to get a certificate from the chief-justice of his colony; this he presented to the governor, who, being satisfied as to the candidate's acquirements, gave him a license. Richard Henderson's self-confidence and genuine talent are exhibited by the story which his brother records, of his attempting to obtain a license to practice law after the brief period of study mentioned above.

Procuring a certificate from the chief-justice he presented himself to the governor of North Carolina as a candidate for a license.

" How long have you read law and what books have you studied? " asked the governor.

" Twelve months," replied young Henderson, naming the books he had used.

The governor replied brusquely that it was wholly unnecessary for him to take the time to give an examination, as no one could in that length of time and with such books become proficient.

" Sir," replied Richard Henderson not a whit dismayed, " I am an applicant for examination; it is your duty to examine me and if found worthy, to grant me a license; if otherwise, to refuse one."

It can well be imagined how quickly the governor bristled up and how mercilessly he would " quiz " a lad who informed him in such a spirited manner what the duties of his office required of him. But the running fire of questions did not daunt the candidate more than had the governor's indifference — and the young Richard received at the close of the interview, not only a license, but what meant more, many encomiums from his governor.

Henderson soon acquired a good practice and became a judge on the bench of the Superior Court. In 1774 the conflict with the British agent in North Carolina was precipitated, and the colonial government was abolished. It was at this time that Judge Henderson became interested in the desire of the Cherokee Indians to sell land. Henderson's plan was to purchase from the Cherokees the great territory lying south of the Kentucky River — one-half the present state of Kentucky. This was quite against the laws and traditions of the only colony which had any valid claim to the territory — Virginia, his native state — but this seemed to matter not to Henderson and his associates; these were John Williams, under whom Henderson had studied law, Leonard Henley Bullock, James Hogg, Nathaniel Thomas, David Hart, John Luttrell, and William Johnstone. At the very beginning of the century Virginia had passed an act forbidding the private purchase of lands from the Indians. The founders of Transylvania evidently doubted Virginia's sweeping claims to the entire interior of the continent — at any rate land companies seemed to be the only means by which the vast wildernesses beyond the mountains could be opened up and settled. Though Virginia soon proved the invalidity of the purchase, she at the same time was frank enough to admit that Henderson's Company had done a good work in giving an impetus to westward expansion, by appropriately recompensing the North Carolinians for their expenditure and labors.

Henderson's purchase was gigantic in its proportions, embracing nearly twenty million acres. The consideration was ten thousand pounds sterling. The purchase was made at the advance settlement at Watauga, March 17, 1775 — only a month before the outbreak at Lexington and Concord. Henderson employed Boone to assist in the transaction, and immediately after engaged him to mark out the road through Cumberland Gap to a settlement in Kentucky, where the Transylvania Company (as Henderson strangely named his organization) was to begin the occupation of the empire it had nominally secured. Of this Boone writes modestly that he was " solicited by a number of North Carolina gentlemen, that were about purchasing the lands lying on the south side of the Kentucky River, from the Cherokee Indians, to attend their treaty at Watauga, in March, 1775, to negotiate with them, and mention the boundaries of the purchase. This I accepted, and at the request of the same gentlemen undertook to mark out a road in the best passage from the settlement through the wilderness to Kentucky, with such assistance as I thought necessary to employ for such an important undertaking." As in the case of Nemacolin's Path across the Alleghenies, so now a second westward Indian pathway was blazed for white man's use; and if the Transylvania Colony can in no other respect be said to have been successful, it certainly conferred an inestimable good upon Virginia and North Carolina and the nation, when it marked out through the hand of Boone the Wilderness Road to Kentucky. From Watauga the path led up to the Gap, where it joined the great Warrior's Path which came down through Kentucky from the Scioto Valley in Ohio. For about fifty miles Boone's Road followed this path northward, whereupon, leaving the Indian trail, Boone bore to the west, marking his course on a buffalo trace toward " Hazel Patch" to the Rockcastle. The buffalo path was followed onward up Roundstone Creek, through "Boone's Gap" in Big Hill; through the present county of Madison, Kentucky; and down little Otter Creek to the Kentucky River. Here Boonesborough was built for the Transylvania Colony, which became the temporary center of Kentucky.

Felix Walker, one of Boone's roadmaking party, made an autobiographical statement about 1824 of this brave attempt to cut a white man's path into Kentucky. From this statement these quotations from De Bow's Review (1854) are pertinent:

" The treaty (at Watauga) being concluded and the purchase made, we proceeded on our journey to meet Col. Daniel Boon, with other adventurers, bound to the same country; accordingly we met and rendezvoused at the Long Island on Holsteen river, united our small force with Colonel Boon and his associates, his brother, Squire Boon, and Col. Richard Callaway, of Virginia. Our company, when united, amounted to 30 persons. We then, by general consent, put ourselves under the management and control of Col. Boon, who was to be our pilot and conductor through the wilderness, to the promised land. . . About the 10th of March we put off from the Long Island, marked out our track with our hatchets, crossed Clinch and Powell's river, over Cumberland mountain, and crossed Cumberland river — came to a watercourse called by Col. — Rockcastle river; killed a fine bear on our way, camped all night and had an excellent supper. On leaving that river, we had to encounter and cut our way through a country of about twenty miles, entirely covered with dead brash, which we found a difficult and laborious task. At the end of which we arrived at the commencement of a cane country, traveled about thirty miles through thick cane and reed, and as the cane ceased, we began to discover the pleasing and rapturous appearance of the plains of Kentucky. A new sky and strange earth seemed to be presented to our view. A sad reverse overtook us two days after, on our way to Kentucky river. On the 25th of March, 1775, we were fired on by the Indians, in our camp asleep, about an hour before day. Capt. Twetty was shot in both knees, and died the third day after. A black man, his body servant, killed dead; myself badly wounded; our company dispersed. So fatal and tragical an event cast a deep gloom of melancholy over all our prospects, and high calculations of long life and happy days in our newly-discovered country were prostrated; hope vanished from the most of us, and left us suspended in the tumult of uncertainty and conjecture. Col. Boon, and a few others, appeared to possess firmness and fortitude. In our calamitous situation, a circumstance occurred one morning after our misfortunes that proved the courage and stability of our few remaining men (for some had gone back). One of our men, who had run off at the fire of the Indians on our camp, was discovered peeping from behind a tree, by a black woman belonging to Colonel Callaway, while gathering some wood. She ran in and gave the alarm of Indians. Colonel Boon instantly caught his rifle, ordered the men to form, take trees, and give battle, and not to run till they saw him fall. They formed agreeably to his directions, and I believe they would have fought with equal bravery to any Spartan band ever brought to the field of action, when the man behind the tree announced his name and came in. . . . . At length I was carried in a litter between two horses, twelve miles, to Kentucky river, where we made a station, and called it Boonsborough, situated in a plain on the south side of the river, wherein was a lick with two sulphur springs strongly impregnated. . . In the sequel and conclusion of my narrative I must not neglect to give honor to whom honor is due. Colonel Boone conducted the company under his care through the wilderness, with great propriety, intrepidity and courage; and was I to enter an exception to any part of his conduct, it would be on the ground that he appeared void of fear and of consequence — too little caution for the enterprise. But let me, with feeling recollection and lasting gratitude, ever remember the unremitting kindness, sympathy, and attention paid to me by Col. Boone in my distress. He was my father, my physician, and friend; he attended me as his child, cured my wounds by the use of medicines from the woods, nursed me with paternal affection until I recovered, without the expectation of reward."

PLAT OF BOONESBOROUGH
[Based on a copy of the original in possession of John Stevens]

It was altogether fitting that among the very first to follow Boone's blazed road to Kentucky we should find Judge Henderson and his fellow-promoters of the Transylvania Company. Nothing shows more plainly the genuineness of their purposes and the heroism of their spirit. They were not foisting on their countrymen a hazardous scheme by which they should profit, while others bore the brunt of the toil and danger. True, Henderson had, purposely or unwittingly, ignored the technicality of Virginia's claim to the possession of the West; but, with an honesty unparalleled at that day in such matters, they met the representatives of the real owners of the lands they desired, and had purchased them and paid down the purchase money. There is almost no doubt that they could have satisfied Virginia's technicalities at a less cost; and then have gone, as so many have done, to fortify their possessions and " fight it out" with the genuine owners of the soil, who would eventually get nothing and lose everything.

This Judge Henderson did not do; nor did he sit down comfortably at home and send others to turn his holdings into money. He arose and started

— amid dangers that shall not be mentioned lest they be minimized — for far-away Kentucky, on the little roadway Boone was opening.

Henderson's party left Fort Watauga March 20, 1775, and arrived at the infant Boonesborough April 20. The leader of the party fortunately kept a record, though meager, of this notable journey. This precious yellow diary is preserved by the Wisconsin Historical Society. It reads:

" Monday March 20th 1775

Having finished my Treaty with the Indians, at Wataugah Sett out for Louisa & arrived at John Shelbeys in the Evening — Tuesday the 21st went to Mr John Seviers in Company of Col° Williams & Col° Hart & staid that day — Wednesday the 22 d — Messrs Williams & Hart set off Home & I staid with M r Sevier Thursday 23 d Still at Mr Seviers — N. B. because our Horses were lost tho. not uneasiy as Messrs Hart and Letteral made a poor Hand of Traveling —

Friday 24th Sett of in pursuit of M r Hart & Letteral. Overtook them Both & Lodged at Capt Bledsoe's —

Satterday the 25th . came to Mrs Callaway's.

Sunday 26th staid there.

Monday 27th Emplied in storeing away Goods.

Tuesday 28th — Sett off for Louisa

Wednesday Continued Journey. N. B. Mr Luttrel not come up.

Thursday 30th Arrived at Capt. Martins in Powels Valey —

Fryday 31st Imploy'd in makeing house to secure the Waggons as we could not possibly clear the road any further. N. B. My Waggon & Saml. Hendersons came up in A. M. W. Luttrel in the Evin'

Satterday the 1 day of April — Imploy'd in making ready for packing & c Mr Hart came up —

Sunday 2nd Continued at Capt. Martins Waiting for the Waggon

Monday the 3rd Still continued Waiting for the Waggon —

Tuesday the 4th — Still continued Waiting for the Waggon. The same evening the Waggon arrived — tho so Late we cood Not proceed —

Wednesday 5th Started off with our pack Horses ab 1 . 3 o'Clock Traveld about 5 Miles to a Large Spring. The Same evening Mr Litteral went out a Hunting & has Not yet returned. [Next. Both Henderson and Sa. Durning went in pursuit of him — erased in diary. The same evening Sam1 . Hendersons & John Farriers Horses took a Scare with there packs Run away with Sams Saddle & Briddle. Farrars Saddle Baggs other things Damaged. Next Morning Sam1. Henderson & Farrar went in pursuit of there Horses. Saddle &c — the same Evening John Farrar returnd to our Camp with News that they had found all there goods. But two of there horses were Missing

Thursday 6 sent John Farrar Back with provission to meet & Assist Sam Henderson with orders to stay with him, till they overtook Us, as we promis'd to wait for them at Cumberland Gap

Fryday the 7th — Sam1. Henderson & John Farrar Returned to us with there Horses Packs & everything safe. We having waited at our Camp 10 miles below Martins for them

[Thursday the 6th — erased]. Traveled about Six Miles to the last Settlement in Powels Valey where we were obliged to stop and kill a Beef wait for Sam Henderson & [N. B?] this was done whilst waiting for Sam1. Henderson as afo[re mentioned]

Fryday the 7th . About Brake of Day begun to snow, About 11 o'Clock received a letter from Mr Littereals camp that were five persons kill'd on the road to the Cantuckee by Indians — Capt. Hart, uppon the receipt of this News Retreated back with his Company & determin'd to Settle in the Valley to make Corn for the Cantuckey People

The same Day Received a Letter from Dan Boone, that his Company was fired uppon by Indians Kill'd Two of his men — tho he kept the ground & saved the Baggage &c.

Satterday the 8th . Started about 10 o'Clock Cross'd Cumberland Gap about 4 Miles Met about 40 persons Returning from the Cantuckey. on Acct. of the Late Murder by the Indians could prevail one one [sic] only to return. Mem° Several Virginians who were with us returned.

Sunday the 9th. Arrived at Cumberland River where we met Robt.Wills & his son returning &c

Monday 10th . Dispach d Capt. Cocke to the Cantukey to Inform Capt. Boone that we were on the road Continued at Camp that day on Acct. of the Badness of the Wether

Tuesday 11th started from Cumberland. made a very good days Travel of Near 20 Mile Kill'd Beef &c.

Wednesday the 12 Travel' d about 5 Miles, prevented going any further by the rains & high water at Richland Creek —

Thursday the 13th . Last Night arrived men [of] our Camp Stewart & ten other men, campt within half mile of us on there Return from Lousia Campt. that Night at Larrel River — they had well nigh turnd three or four of our Virg & us back.

Fryday the 14. Traveld about 12 Miles to a Camp &c

Satterday the 15th . Traveld about 18 Miles & campt on the North side of Rock Castle River. — this River's a fork of Cumberland — lost an ax this morn at Camp.

Sunday the 16th . About 12 oClock Met Jemes McAfee with 18 other persons Returning from Cantuckey Traveld about 22 Miles and Campt on the head of Dicks River where Luna from McAfees camp came to us resolved to go to the Louisa —

Monday 17th Started about 3 o'Clock prevented by Rain. Traveld 7 Miles

Tuesday the 18th . Traveld about 16 Miles, met Michael Stoner with Pack Horses to assist us. Campt that Night in the Edge of the Rich Land — Stoner brought us Excellent Beef in plenty

Wednesday 19th . Traveld about 16 Miles Campt on Oter Creek — a good mill place

Thursday the 20th . Arrived at Fort Boone, on the Mouth of Oter Creek Cantukey River — where we were Saluted by a running fire of about 25 Guns; all that was then at Fort — The men appeared in high Spirits & much rejoiced on our arrival "

Colonel Henderson (as the leader of the Transylvania Colony is best known) arrived at Boonesborough one day after the outbreak of the Revolutionary struggle at Lexington and Concord, and on his own fortieth birthday.

A clearer glimpse of the fortunes of this company of pilgrims who followed in Boone's wake is preserved for us in the journal kept by William Calk, who was with Hart's party that Henderson met at Martin's cabin on the second of April. The original manuscript is in the possession of the family of the late Mr. Thomas Calk, near Mt. Sterling, Kentucky.

It reads:

"1775 Mond. 13th — I set out from prince wm. to travel to caintuck on tuefday Night our company all got together at Mr. Prifes on rapadan which was Abraham hanks philip Drake Eaneck Smith Robert Whitledge & my Self, thear Abrams Dogs leg got Broke By Drake's Dog.

Wedns. 15th, — We started early from prifes made a good Days travel & lodge this night at Mr. Cars on North fork James River.

Thurs. 16th, — We started early it raind Chief part of the Day Snowd in the Eavening very hard & was very Coald we traveld all Day & got to Mr. Blacks at the foot of the Blue Ridge.

fryd. 17th — We start early crofs the Ridge the wind Blows very hard & cold and lodge at James loyls.

Satrd. 18th — We git this Day to William Anderfons at Crows ferrey & there we Stay till monday morning.

Mond. 20th — We start early crofs the fery and lodge this night at Wm. Adamfes on the head of Catauby.

tuefd. 21 st — We start early and git over pepers ferey on new river & lodge at pepers this night.

Wedns 22d — We start early and git to foart Chifsel whear we git some good loaf Bread & good whifkey.

thurs 23d — we start early & travel till a good while in the Night and git to major Cammels on holfton River.

fryday 24th — we start early & turn out of the wagon Road to go acrofs the mountains to go by Danil Smiths we loof e Driver Come to a turabel mountain that tired us all almost to death to git over it & we lodge this night on the Lawrel fork of holfton under agrait mountain & Roaft a fine fat turkey for our suppers & Eat it without aney Bread.

Satrd 25th — We start early travel over Some more very Bad mountains one that is caled Clinch mountain & we git this night to Danil Smiths on Clinch and there we staid till thurfday morning on tuefday night & wednefday morning it snowd Very hard and was very Coald & we hunted a good deal there while we staid in Rough mountains and kild three deer & one turkey Eanock Abram & I got loft tuefday night & it a snowing & Should a lain in the mountains had not had a pocket compas By which I got in a littel in the night and fired guns and they heard them and cairn in By the Repoart.

thursd 30th — We set out again & went down to Elk gardin and there suplid our Selves With Seed Corn & irish tators then we went on a littel way I turnd my hors to drive afore me & he got scard ran away threw Down the Saddel Bags and broke three of our powder goards & Abrams beaft Burft open a walet of corn & lost a good Deal & made a turrabel fluftration amongft the Reaft of the Horfes Drakes mair run againft a fapling & noct it down we cacht them all agin & went on & lodgd at John Duncans.

fryd 31st — We Suployd our Selves at Dunkans with a 108 pounds of Bacon & went on again to Brileys mill & suployd our Selves with meal & lodged this night on Clinch By a large cainbraike & cuckt our Suppers.

April Satrd firft — this morning there is ice at our camp half inch thick we start early & travel this Day along a verey Bad hilley way crofs one creek whear the horfes almoft got mired some fell in & all wet their loads we crofs Clinch River & travell till late in the Night & camp on Cove creek having two men with us that wair pilates.

Sund 2d — this morning is a very hard frost we Start early travel over powels mountain and camp in the head of Powels valey whear there is verey good food.

mond 3d We Start early travel down the valey crofs powels River go some throu the woods without aney track crofs some Bad hils git into henderfons Road camp on a creek in powels valey.

Tuefday 4th Raney, we Start about 10 oclock and git down to Capt. martins in the valey where we over take Coin henderfon & his Companey Bound for Caintuck & there we camp this Night there they were Broiling & Eating Beef without Bread.

Wednefday 5th Breaks away fair & we go on down the valey & camp on indian Creek we had this creek to crofs maney times & very Bad Banks Abrams saddel turnd & the load all fell in we go out this Eavening & kill two Deer.

thurs 6th this morning is ahard frost & we wait at Camp for Coin henderfon & companey to come up they come up about 12 o'clock & we join with them and camp there Still this night waiting for some part of the companey that had thier horfes ran away with their packs.

fryday 7th this morning is a very hard snowey morning we still continue at Camp Being in number about 40 men & Some neagros this Eaven — Comes a letter from Capt. Boone at caintuck of the indians doing mifchief and some turns back.

1775

Satrd April 8th — We all pact up and started croft Cumberland gap about one o'clock this Day We Met a great maney peopel turned Back for fear of the indians but our Companey goes on Still with good courage we come to a very ugly Creek with steep Banks & have it to crofs several times on this Creek we camp this night.

Sunday 9th — this morning we wait at camp for the cattle to Be drove up to kill a Beef tis late Before they come & peopel makes out alittel snack & agree to go on till Night we git to Cumberland River & there we camp meet 2 more men turn Back.

Monday 10th — this is alowry morning & very like for Rain & we keep at Camp this day and some goes out ahunting. I & two more goes up avery large mountain Near the tops we faw the track of two indians & whear they had lain unter some Rocks some of the companey went over the River a bofelo hunting but found None at night Capt. hart comes up with his packs & there they hide some of thier lead to lighten thier packs that they may travel faster.

tuefday 11th — this is a very loury morning & like for Rain But we all agree to start Early we crofs Cumberland River & travel Down it about 10 miles through Some turrabel cainbrakes as we went down abrams mair ran into the River with Her load & Swam over he folowd her & got on her & made her Swim Back agin it is a very raney Eavening we take up Camp near Richland Creek they kill a beef Mr. Drake Bakes Bread without wafhing his hands we Keep Sentry this Night for fear of the indians.

Wednefday 12th this is a Raney morning But we pack up & go on we come to Richland Creek it is high we toat our packs over on a tree & swim our horfes over & there we meet another Companey going Back they tell such News Abram & Drake is afraid to go aney further there we camp this night.

thurfday 13th this morning the weather Seems to breake & Be fair Abram & Drake turn Back we go on & git to loral River we come to a creek Before wheare we are able to unload & toate our packs over on a log this day we meet about 20 more turning Back we are obligd to toat our packs over loral river & swim our horfes one hors Ran in with his pack & loft it in the River & they got it agin.

fryday 14th — this is a clear morning with a smart froft we go on & have a very mire Road and camp this Night on a creek of loral River and are surprisd at camp By a wolf.

Satterday 15th clear with a Small froft we start early we meet Some men that turns & goes With us we travel this Day through the plais caled the Brefsh & crofs Rockcafs River & camp ther this Night & have fine food for our horfes.

Sunday 16th — cloudy & warm we start early & go on about 2 mile down the River and then turn up a creek that we croft about 50 times Some very bad foards with a great Deal of very good land on it in the Eavening we git over to the waters of Caintuck & go a littel Down the creek & there we camp keep sentry the forepart of the night it Rains very har all night.

monday 17th this is a very rany morning But breaks about a 11 oclock & we go on and camp this Night in several companeys on Some of the creeks of Caintuck.

tuefday 18th fair & cool and we go on about 10 oclock we meet 4 men from Boons camp that cairn to cunduck us on we camp this night juft on the Begining of the good land near the Blue lick they kill 2 bofelos this Eavening.

Wednesd 19th Smart froft this morning they kill 3 bofelos about 11 oclock we come to where the indians fired on Boons company & kild 2 men & a dog & wounded one man in the thigh we campt this night on oter creek.

thurfday 20th this morning is clear and cool. We start early and git Down to caintuck to Boons foart about 12 o'clock wheare we stop they come out to meet us & welcom us in with a voley of guns.

fryday 21st warm this Day they Begin laying off lots in the town and prearing for peopel to go to worck to make corn.

Satterday 22 nd they finifh laying out lots this Eavening I went a-fishing and cactht 3 cats they meet in the night to Draw for choise of lots but refer it till morning

1775

Sunday April 23d this morning the peopel meets & Draws for chois of loots this is a very warm day.

monday 24th We all view our loots & Some Dont like them about 12 oclock the Combfes come to town & Next morning they make them a bark canew and Set off down the River to meet their Companey.

tuesday 25th in the eavening we git us a plaife at the mouth of the creek & begin clearing.

Wednefday 26th We Begin Building us a house & a plaife of Defense to Keep the indians off this day we Begin to live without Bread.

thurfday 27th Raney all Day But We Still keep about our houfe.

Satterday 29th — We git our houfe kivered with Bark & move our things into it at Night and Begin houfkeeping Eanock Smith Robert Whitledge & my Self.

May, Monday firft I go out to look for my mair and saw 4 bufelos the Being the firft that I Saw & I shot one of them but did not git him when I cairn Home Eanock & Robin had found the mair & was gone out a hunting & did Not come in for — Days and kild only one Deer.

tuefday 2d I went out in the morning & kild a turkey and come in & got some on for my breakfaft and then went & Sot in to clearing for Corn."

The personal statement of Mrs. Elizabeth Thomas is of interest in this connection. She was one of Col. Calloway's company that followed Henderson in September 1775. This statement is preserved in the library of the Wisconsin Historical Society and reads:

" I was born in Virginia on the 4th day of Sept 1764. In Rockbridge county near the Natural Bridge my father moved on the North Fork of Holston within 4 or 5 miles of Abbingdon & remained there two or three years and in March 1775 we moved down Holstien near the Big Island, [Long Island] where we remained until Sept 1775 when Col Calloway and his company came along going to Kentucky, when my father William Pogue packed up and came with him with our family, Col Boone and with his wife and family and Col Hugh Mcgary, Thomas Denton and Richard Hogan were on the road before us and when we arrived at Boonesborough the latter part of September There was only fur [four] or six cabbins built along on the Bank of the Kentucky river but not picketted in being open on two sides."

This was the great pathway of early pioneers to Kentucky, and the course of the marvelous floodtide of immigration which swept over the mountains in the last three decades of the eighteenth century.

The itineraries of early travelers describe the Wilderness Road in definite terms. One of the earliest is that given by John Filson, whose history of Kentucky was published as early as 1784. It described the route from Philadelphia to Louisville (eight hundred and twenty-six miles), as follows:

Distance in Miles

From Philadelphia to Lancaster, 66

To Wright's on the Susquehanna, 10

To Yorktown, 12

To Abbotstown, 15

To Hunterstown, 10

To mountain at Black's Gap, 3

To other side of the mountain, 7

To Stone-house Tavern, 25

To Wadkin's Ferry on Potomac, 14

To Martinsburg, 13

To Winchester, 13

To Newtown, 8

To Stoverstown, 10

To Woodstock, 12

To Shenandoah River, 15

To North Branch Shenandoah, 29

To Staunton, 15
To North Fork James River, 37
To Botetourt C. H., 12
To Woods on Catawba River, 21
To Paterson.s. on Roanoke, 9
To Alleghany Mountain, 8
To New River, 12
To Forks of Road, 16
To Fort Chissel, 12
To Stone Mill, 11
To Boyds, 8
To Head of Holstein, 5
To Washington C. H., 45
To the Block-house, 35
To Powell Mountain, 33
To Walden's Ridge, 3
To Valley Station, 4
To Martin's Cabin, 25
To Cumberland Mountain, 20
To Cumberland River, 13
To Flat Lick, 9
To Stinking Creek, 2
To Richland Creek, 7
Down Richland Creek, 8
To Racoon Spring,6
To Laurel River, 2
To Hazel Patch, 15
To Rockcastle River, 10
To English Station, 25
To Col. Edward's Crab Orchard, 3
To Whitley's Station, 5
To Logan's Station, 5
To Clark's Station, 7
To Crow's Station, 4
To Harrod's Station, 3
To Harlands', 4
To Harbisons, 10
To Bardstown, 25
To Salt Works, 25
To Falls of the Ohio, 20
Total: 826

Mr. Speed preserves for us the itinerary with "observations and occurrences" of William Brown, the father of Judge Alfred M. Brown, of Elizabethtown, Kentucky. "It is contained in a small manuscript book," writes Mr. Speed, " which has been preserved in the family. It is especially interesting from the fact that immediately upon his arrival in Kentucky, by the journey of which he made a complete record, the Battle of Blue Licks occurred. He aided in burying the slain, among whom was his own brother, James Brown." The itinerary and " observations and occurrences " follow:

(1782) " Hanover to Richmond, Henrico Co., 18

To Widow Simpson's, Chesterford, . 14

To Powhatan Co. House, . . .16

To Joseph Thompson's at the forks of the road, 8

To Long's Ordinary, Buckingham, . 9

To Hoolen's on Willis Creek, . . 8

To Mrs. Sanders, Cumberland, . . 3

To Widow Thompson's passing Hood's and Swiney's, ... 27

To Captain Hunter's, ... 5

To Thompson's on the Long Mo., Campbell, 5

To Dupriest, 6

To New London, 10

To Liberty Town, 16

To Yearley's, at Goose Creek, Bedford, 12

To M. Loland, at the Blue Ridge Gap, 6

To Big Flat Lick, 10

To Fort Lewis, Botetourt, . . .12

To Hans' Meadows, ... 20

To English's Ferry, New River, . . 12

To Fort Chiswell, 30

To Atkins' Ordinary, . . . -19

To Mid Fork Holstein —

To Cross White's, Montgomery, . . 3

To Col. Arthur Campbell's, ... 3

To 7-mile Ford of Holstein, ... 6

To Maj. Dysart's Mill, ...12

To Washington Co. House, ... 10

To Head of Reedy Creek, Sullivan Co., North Carolina, ... 20

To Block House, ...13

To North Fork Holstein, ... 2

To Moccasin Gap, 5

To Clinch River, 11

To Ford of Stock Creek, ... 2

To Little Flat Lick,

To North Fork of Clinch, 5

To Powell's Mountain, 1
To Wallan Ridge, 1
To Valley Station, 5
To Powell's River, 2
To Glade Spring, 4
To Martin's Station, 19
To Big Spring, 12
To Cumberland Mountain Gap, 8
To Yellow Creek, 2
To Cumberland River,13
To Big Flat Lick, 9
To Little Richland Creek, 10
To Big Richland Creek, 1
To Robinson Creek, 10
To Raccoon Spring, 1
To Laurel River, 2
To Little Laurel River, 5
To Raccoon Creek, 8
To Hazel Patch, 4
To Rockcastle Creek, 6
To Rockcastle River, 7
To Scaggs' Creek, 5
To Head of Dicks River, 15
To English Station, 8
To Crab Orchard, 3
To Logan's Old Fort, ...11
To Doehurty's Station, ... 8
To Harrod's Station, ... 6
To Harrodsburg, 6
From Hanover to Harrodsburg is 555 miles.

Observations and Occurrences: Set Out from Hanover Monday, 27th May, 1782; arrived at the Block-house about the first week in July. The road from Hanover to this place is generally very good; crossing the Blue Ridge is not bad; there is not more than a small hill with some winding to go over. Neither is the Alleghany Mountain by any means difficult at this gap. There are one or two high hills about New River and Fort Chiswell. The ford of New River is rather bad; therefore we thought it advisable to cross in the ferryboat. This is generally a good-watered road as far as the Block-house. We waited hereabouts near two weeks for company, and then set out for the wilderness with twelve men and ten guns, this being Thursday, 18th July. The road from this until you get over Wallen's Ridge generally is bad, some part very much so, particularly about Stock Creek and Stock Creek Ridge. It is a very mountainous country hereabout, but there is some fine land in the bottoms, near the watercourses, in narrow slips. It will be but a thin settled country whenever it is settled. The fords of Holstein and Clinch are both good in dry weather, but in a rainy season you are often obliged to raft over. From them along down Powell's Valley until you get to Cumberland Gap is pretty good; this valley is formed by Cumberland Mountain on the northwest, and Powell Mountain on the southeast, and appears to bear from northeast southwestwardly, and is, I suppose, about one hundred miles in length, and from ten to twelve miles in breadth. The land generally is good, and is an exceeding well-watered country, as well as the country on Holstein River, abounding with fine springs and little brooks. For about fifty miles, as you travel along the valley, Cumberland Mountain appears to be a very high ridge of white rocks, inaccessible in most places to either man or beast, and affords a wild, romantic prospect. The way through the gap is not very difficult, but from its situation travelers may be attacked in some places, crossing the mountain, by the enemy to a very great disadvantage. From thence until you pass Rockcastle River there is very little good road; this tract of country is very mountainous, and badly watered along the trace, especially for springs. There is some good land on the water-courses, and just on this side Cumberland River appears to be a good tract, and within a few years I expect to have a settlement on it. Some parts of the road are very miry in rainy weather. The fords of Cumberland and Rockcastle are both good unless the waters be too high; after you cross Rockcastle there are a few high hills, and the rest of the way tolerable good; the land appears to be rather weak, chiefly timbered with oak, etc. The first of the Kentucky waters you touch upon is the head of Dick's River, just eight miles from English's. Here we arrived Thursday, 25th inst., which is just seven days since we started from the Block-house. Monday, 29th inst., I got to Harrodsburg, and saw brother James. The next day we parted, as he was about setting off on a journey to Cumberland.

On Monday, August 19th, Colonel John Todd, with a party of one hundred and eighty-two of our men, attacked a body of Indians, supposed to number six or seven hundred, at the Blue Lick, and was defeated, with the loss of sixty-five persons missing and slain.

Officers lost: Colonels — John Todd and Stephen Trigg; Majors — Edward Bulger and Silas Harlan; Captains — W. McBride, John Gordon, Jos. Kincaid, and Clough Overton; Lieutenants — W. Givens, and John Kennedy; Ensign — John McMurtry.

In this action brother James fell. On Saturday 24th inst., Colonel Logan, with four hundred and seventy men, went on the battle-ground and buried the slain; found on the field, slain, forty-three men, missing, twenty-two, in all sixty-five.

I traveled but little about the country. From English's to Harrodsburg was the farthest west, and from Logan's Fort to the Blue Lick the farthest north. Thus far the land was generally good — except near and about the Lick it was very poor and badly timbered — generally badly watered, but pretty well timbered. At Richmond Ford, on the Kentucky River, the bank a little below the ford appears to be largely upward of a hundred feet perpendicular of rock.

On my return to Hanover I set off from John Craigs' Monday, 23rd September, 1782; left English's Tuesday, 1 o'clock, arrived at the Block-house the Monday evening following, and kept on the same route downward chiefly that I traveled out. Nothing material occurred to me. Got to Hanover sometime about the last of October the same year."

Thomas Speed's grandfather gives the following itinerary from " Charlotte Court House to Kentucky " under date of 1790:

Distance in Miles

" From Charlotte Court-House to Campbell Court-House, 41
To New London, 13
To Colonel James Callaway's 3
To Liberty, 13
To Colonel Flemming's, 28
To Big Lick, 2
To Mrs. Kent's, 20
To English's Ferry, 20
To Carter's, 13
To Fort Chissel, 12
To the Stone-mill, 11
To Adkins', 16
To Russell Place, 16
To Greenaway's, 14
To Washington Court-House, 6
To the Block -house, 35
To Farriss's, 5
To Clinch River, 12
To Scott's Station, 12
To Cox's at Powell River, 10
To Martin's Station, 2
To — [manuscript defaced]
To Cumberland Mountain, 3
To Cumberland River, 15
To Flat Lick, 9
To Stinking Creek, 2
To Richland Creek, 7
To Raccoon Spring, 14
To Laurel River, 2
To Hazel Patch, 15
To Rockcastle, 10
To — [manuscript defaced].

The foregoing itineraries afford us some conception of the settlements and " improvements " that sprang up along the winding thoroughfare from Virginia to Kentucky. The writer has sought with some care to know more of these — of the modes of travel, the entertainment which was afforded along the road to men and beasts, and the social relation of the greater settlements in Virginia and Kentucky to this thin line of human lives across the continent. Very little information has been secured. It is plain that the great immigration to Kentucky would have been out of the question had there been no means of succor and assistance along the road. There were many who gained their livelihood as pioneer innkeepers and provisioned along Boone's Road. Among the very few of these of whom any record is left, Captain Joseph Martin is perhaps the most prominent and most worthy of remembrance. Martin's "cabin" or "station," as it is variously termed, occupied a strategic point in far-famed Powell's Valley, one hundred and eighty miles west of Inglis Ferry, twenty miles east of Cumberland Gap and about one hundred and thirty miles southeast of Crab Orchard and Boonesborough. Captain Martin was Virginia Agent for Indian affairs, and was the most prominent man in the scattered settlements in Powell's Valley, where he was living at the time of the founding of Boonesborough. Later he made his headquarters at Long Island in North Carolina. It is plain from Colonel Henderson's journal that wagons could proceed along Boone's Road in 1775 no further than Martin's cabin. Here everything was transferred to the packhorses. Several letters from Colonel Henderson to Captain Martin, preserved by the Wisconsin Historical Society, give us a glimpse of silent Powell's Valley. One of them reads:

" Boonesborough 12th June 1775 Dear Sir:

Mr Ralph Williams, David Burnay, and William Mellar will apply to you for salt and other things which we left with you and was sent for us since we came away — Please to deliver to them, or those they may employ what they ask for, and take a receipt — Also write me a few lines informing me, what you have sent &c by hem & by whom — I long much to hear from you, pray write me at Large, how the matter goes with you in the valey, as well as what passes in Virginia — If the packhorsemen should want anything towards securing my books from Damage packsaddles, provisions, or any thing which you see is necessary; please to let them have it on our ace 1 . — All things goes well hitherto with us, I hope the[y] do with you would have sent your Mares but am afraid they are not done horsing They will be safely brought by my brother in a few weeks I am Dear Sir your

Hble Servt.

Richd. Henderson

Mr Joseph Martin in the Valley "

On July 20 he wrote again:

" Am sorry to hear that the People in the valey are distressed for provisions and ammunition have given some directions to my brother to assist you a little with Powder.

Standly, I suppose has before now delivered your Inglish mare, and the other you'l receive by my brother — when we meet will render an ace 1 , for my behaviour in Keeping them so long — We did not forget you at the time of making Laws, your part of the Country is too remote from ours to attend our Convention you must have Laws made by an Assembly of your own, I have prepared a plan which I hope you'l approve but more of that when we meet which I hope will be soon, tho 'til Col. Boone comes cant say when — Am extreamly sorry for the affair with the Indians on the 23rd of last month. I wish it may not have a bad effect, but will use my endeavors to find out who they were & have the matter settled — your spirited conduct gives me great Pleasure — Keep your men in heart if possible, now is our time, the Indians must not drive us — depend upon it that the Chief men and warriors of the Cherokees will not countenance what there men attempted and will punish them — Pray my Dear Sir don't let any person settle Lower down the valey I am affraid they are now too low & must come away I did not want any person to settle yet below Cumberland gap — My Brother will [tell] you of the news of these parts — in haste Dear Sir . ."

In December, John Williams wrote Captain Martin from Boonesborough and his letter gives us a closer insight into affairs along Boone's Road:

" . . With respect to the complaints of the inhabitants of Powells Valley with regard to cattle being lodged there, I should think it altogether unjust than [that] non-inhabitants should bring in cattle to destroy and eat up the range of the inhabitants' stock; Yet, Sir, I cannot conceive that Col. Hart's stopping his stock there, when on their way here, to recruit them for their journey, can be the least infringement. Col. Hart is a proprietor, & [has] as great a right in the country as any one man. In the Valley are many lands yet unentered; and certainly if there be a right in letting stock into the range, he has a right equal to any man alive. I therefore hope you will endeavor to convince the inhabitants thereof, and that it is no indulgence to Col. Hart, but a right he claims, and what I think him justly entitled to.

I hope to have the pleasure of seeing you at Boonesborough the 21st instant — in the meantime making not the least doubt but that you will use every justifiable Method in Keeping up peace and harmony in the Valley"

As indicated in the former letter, the emigrants from the colonies were encroaching upon the Cherokee lands beyond the Henderson purchase. Joseph Martin was under the necessity of protesting to the Assembly of North Carolina against settlers from that state pressing beyond the Henderson lands and settling in the Cherokee country. It is seen by Colonel Henderson's letter that Boone's Road marked the most westerly limit to which pioneers could go with safety. Irresponsible Cherokees invaded the

Henderson purchase, and equally irresponsible (or ignorant) whites invaded the Cherokee country. The difficulty probably lay in not having a definite, plain boundary line that he who ran might recognize.

The settlement here in Powell's Valley meant everything to the pioneers of Kentucky. This is made additionally plain by the attempt of interested parties to have Captain Martin's Indian Agency removed from Long Island to a point on Boone's Road near Cumberland Gap. In December 1782 William Christian wrote Governor Harrison from " Great [Long] Island," explaining the dependence of the inhabitants (undoubtedly both red and white) upon Martin in time of need. " I find," he wrote, " that the party here, consisting of fifty odd, are living on Col. Martin's corn. Whenever a family begins to be in a starving condition, it is very probable they will push for this place & throw themselves upon him for bread."

Fourteen days later he wrote from Mahanaim to " Hon. Col. Sampson Matthews " of Richmond; protesting against Virginia's Indian Agency being kept at Long Island, North Carolina; and urging that it be removed to near Cumberland Gap:

" The Gap is near half way betwixt our settlements on Holston and Kentucky, and a post there would be a resting place for our poor citizens going back and forward, and would be a great means of saving the lives of hundreds of them. For it seldom happens that Indians will kill people near where they trade; & it is thereabouts the most of the mischief on the road has been done. . . I view the change I propose as of great importance to the frontier of Washington, [County] to our people journeying to & from Kentucky, particularly the poor families moving out. . . "

It was, throughout the eighteenth century, exceedingly dangerous to travel Boone's Road; and those who journeyed either way joined together and traveled in " companies." Indeed there was risk enough for the most daring, in any case; but a well-armed "company" of tried pioneers on Boone's Road was a dangerous game upon which to prey. It was customary to advertise the departure of a company either from Virginia or Kentucky, in local papers; in order that any desiring to make the journey might know of the intended departure. The principal rendezvous in Kentucky was the frontier settlement of Crab Orchard. Certain of these advertisements are extremely interesting; the verbal changes are significant if closely read:

Notice
is hereby given, that a company will meet at the Crab Orchard, on Sunday the 4th day of May, to go through the wilderness, and to set out on the 5th at which time most of the Delegates to the state convention will go

A large company will meet at the Crab orchard on Sunday the 25th of May, in order to make an early start on Monday the 26th through the wilderness for the old settlement

A large company will meet at the Crab Orchard on the 15th day of May, in readiness to start on the 16th through the Wilderness for Richmond

Notice

Is hereby given that several gentlemen propose meeting at the Crab-orchard on the 4th of June in perfect readiness to move early the next morning through the Wilderness

Notice

A large company will meet at the Crab-Orchard the 19th of November in order to start the next day through the Wilderness. As it is very dangerous on account of the Indians, it is hoped each person will go well armed. It appears that unarmed persons sometimes attached themselves to companies and relied on others to protect them in times of danger. One advertisement urged that everyone should go armed and " not to depend on others to defend them." The frequency of the departure of such companies suggests the great amount of travel on Boone's Road. As early as 1788 parties were advertised to leave Crab Orchard May 5, May 15, May 26, June 4, and June 16. Nor does it seem that there was much abatement during the more inclement (safer?) months; in the fall of the same year companies were advertised to depart November 19, December 9, and December 19. Yet at this season the Indians were often out waylaying travelers — driven no doubt by hunger to deeds of desperation. The sufferings of such red-skinned marauders have found little place in history; but they are, nevertheless, particularly suggestive. One story, which has not perhaps been told ad nauseam, is to the point; and would be amusing if it were not so fatally conclusive. In the winter of 1787-88 a party on Boone's Road was attacked by Indians not far from the Kentucky border. Their horses were plundered of goods, but the travelers escaped. Hurrying "in" to the settlements a company was raised to make a pursuit. By their tracks in the snow the Indians were accurately followed. They were overtaken at a camp, where they were drying their blankets, &c, before a great fire. At the first charge the savages, completely surprised, took to their heels — stark naked. Not satisfied with recovering the stolen goods the Kentuckians pursued the fugitives into the mountains. Along the course they found trees stripped of pieces of bark, with which the Indians had attempted to cover their bodies. They were not overtaken, though some of their well-protected pursuers had their own feet frost-bitten. The awful fate of the savages is unquestionable.

Before Richard Henderson arrived in Kentucky Daniel Boone wrote him: " My advice to you, sir, is to come or send as soon as possible. Your company is desired greatly, for the people are very uneasy, but are willing to stay and venture their lives with you, and now is the time to illustrate the intentions of the Indians, and keep the country whilst we are in it. If we give way to them now, it will ever be the case."

This letter shows plainly how the best-informed man in Kentucky regarded Henderson's settlement at Boonesborough. Henderson's purchase was repudiated by both Virginia and North Carolina; but the Virginia Legislature confirmed Henderson's sales of land, in so far as they were made to actual settlers, and not to speculators. Henderson and his associates were granted land in lieu of that taken from them. The Transylvania Company, while looked upon askance by many who preferred to risk their tomahawk claim rights to those the Company granted, exerted as great a moral influence in the first settlement of Kentucky as Daniel Boone affirmed it would — a greater influence than any other company before the Revolutionary War.

What it meant to the American colonies to have a brave band of pioneers in Kentucky at that crucial epoch, is an important chapter in the history of Boone's Road.

CHAPTER IV - KENTUCKY IN THE REVOLUTION

HISTORY was fast being made in Kentucky when the Revolutionary struggle reached the crisis in 1775 at Concord and Lexington. South of the Ohio River Virginia's new empire was filling with the conquerors of the West. The Mississippi Valley counted a population of thirteen thousand, three thousand being the population of New Orleans. St. Louis, in Spanish possession, was carrying on a brisk trade with the Indians on the Missouri. Vincennes, the British port on the Wabash, had a population of four hundred whites. Detroit, the metropolis of the West, numbered fifteen hundred inhabitants, more than double the number in the dashing days of Gladwin only a decade before. The British flag also waved at Kaskaskia on the Mississippi, and at Sandusky. This fringe of British forts on the north was separated from the American metropolis of the West, Pittsburg, and from the first fortresses built in Kentucky, by leagues of forests, dark as when Bouquet pierced them; and filled with sullen Indian nations, awed for the time being by Dunmore's invasion, but silently biding their time to avenge themselves for the loss of the meadow lands of Ken-ta-kee.

Such was the condition of affairs when, in April 1775, the open struggle for independence of the American colonies was roughly precipitated at Lexington. It might seem to the casual observer that the colonists, who were now hastening by way of Boone's Wilderness Road into the Virginian Kentucky, could not feel the intense jealousy for American interests which was felt by the patriots in the East. On the contrary, there is evidence that these first pioneers into the West had a profound knowledge of the situation; and a sympathy for the struggling patriots, which was enhanced even by the distance which separated them, and the hardships they had endured. Not a few of them, too, had known personally of the plundering British officials and the obnoxious taxes. It is the proud boast of Kentuckians that in the center of their beautiful Blue Grass country was erected the first monument to the first dead of the Revolution. A party of pioneers heard the news of the Battle of Lexington while sitting about their camp fire. Long into the night the rough men told and retold the news, and before morning named the new settlement they were to make, Lexington, in honor of New England's dead.

It was not at all evident at first what the war was going to amount to in the West. Scarcely more was known in the West of the Revolutionary War than had been known two decades before of the French and Indian War. But at the outset it was plain that there was to be a tremendous struggle on both sides to gain the allegiance, as the British desired, of the Indian nations which lay between the Ohio River and the Great Lakes. For two years the struggle in the East went on, engrossing the entire attention of both parties. During 1776 and 1777 the history of the West is merely the continuation of the bloody story of the years which led up to Dunmore's campaign, like the savage attack on Wheeling, in September, 1777. Slowly the Indians forgot

Lewis's crushing victory at Point Pleasant, and their solemn pledges at Camp Charlotte; and were raiding the feeble Kentucky posts with undiminished relish, or giving the Long Knives plenty of provocation for the barbarities of which the latter are known to have been guilty.

The opening scene of the Revolutionary War in the West was the most important phase of the war in the history of Boone's Wilderness Road; for at the very outset the question was decided once for all whether or not that thin, long, priceless path to Kentucky through the Watauga settlement was to be held or lost. If it could not be held, there was no hope left for the brave men who had gone to found that western empire beyond the Cumberland Mountains. With their line of retreat cut in two by the southern Indians, they were left without hope of succor or success: for the success of their enterprise depended upon the inspiration their advance gave to those behind them. None would come if the Wautauga settlement did not survive. The British agents among the Southern Indians — the Cherokees, Creeks, Choctaws and Chickasaws — precipitated a quick and early struggle along this historic pathway by goading the Indians into a murderous attack upon the Watauga settlement. The Cherokees who had sold the Transylvania Company its lands, were the most easily incited to war, and fifty packhorse loads of ammunition scattered through their towns in those deep mountain valleys where the two Carolinas and Georgia meet, determined an outburst in July, 1776. Straight north from them lay the rude beginnings of civilization on the headwaters of the Tennessee, and further "in" was the frontier line of Virginia. The headquarters of the Watauga settlement may be said to have been Fort Watauga, commanded by the heroes Robertson and Sevier; here Boone had made the treaty with the Cherokees for Richard Henderson, a trifle over a year ago. Eaton's, Evan Shelby's, John Shelby's, Campbell's, and the Wommack forts were the important way stations on this path from Virginia to Kentucky. Two Indian parties larger than the others made for Fort Watauga and Eaton's Station, and the defenders of the latter post, learning from their scouts that a formidable array under the notorious Dragging Canoe was coming, resolved to give them a hot, unexpected welcome. Accordingly, on the morning of July twentieth nearly two hundred brown forms could have been seen stealing away from the fort in two thin lines half lost in the fog toward the open land known as "the Flats" near the " Long Island" of the Holston. In the march an advance party of a score of savages was met and put to flight. No other signs of the enemy could be discovered and the men started back to their fort at the end of the day.

Dragging Canoe, not less audacious than his foes, awaited his time, and when the whites were marching homeward, came down upon them, his savages forming a wedge-shaped line of battle. Instantly the borderers fell back to the right and left, and with a desperate quietness awaited the onslaught. The Indian plan of rushing the whites off their feet by an overwhelming charge failed; the borderers settled deeper into the ground and met the rush and dashed the savage line into fragments. One charge — and all was over. There was no recovering from this form of attack for untrained soldiery, and the assaulting band instantly broke and fled. This battle of Long Island Flats was the first of the series of victories for the Watauga pioneers; its importance can hardly be measured today.

Its best fruit was that it brought other victories to the encouraged Wataugans. On the same day the other Indian horde invested and assailed Fort Watauga at dawn. Only about two score men were at home to defend a large number of women and children, but they were fully equal to the emergency and with a frightful burst of fire drove back the line of savages which could just be seen advancing at that hour when Indians invariably made their attacks — the early dawn. Robertson was senior officer in command, and Sevier his brave assistant. The latter, having learned of the Indian uprising, characteristically wrote a message to the people far away on the Virginia border to look well to their homes — never even asking that assistance be sent to the much more feeble and vastly more endangered Watauga settlement on the Kentucky road.

Elsewhere the border warfare was being waged with varying fortune; a small band of Georgian frontiersmen invaded the Cherokee country in the hope of capturing a notorious British agent, Cameron; it suffered heavily through the faithlessness of the Cherokees. The whole southern frontier was aroused, and plans for dashes into the Cherokee country were made but could not be forwarded simultaneously. Yet Cameron and his Tories and Indians acted in unison and brought sudden desolation into South Carolina. The force of the blow was broken by the brave Colonel Andrew Williamson, who, gathering over a thousand volunteers near the end of July began the first important invasion of the Cherokee country. Near Eseneka, the Cherokee town, the Carolinians found Cameron and won a costly victory. After some internal dissensions the little army got on its mettle and went steadily forward to wipe out the lower Cherokee towns, which was completely accomplished by the middle of August. Scarcity of ammunition, only, kept Williamson from attacking the middle towns.

This task fell to the lot of the second expedition into the Cherokee country. This was a joint campaign waged by North and South Carolina, and Virginia, each to furnish two thousand men. The North Carolinians under Rutherford were earliest in the field. This officer with twenty-four hundred men left the head of the Catawba and opened " Rutherford's Trace " leading to Swananoa Gap in the Blue Ridge and on to the middle Cherokee towns by way of Warrior's Ford of French Broad and Mount Cowee. The middle towns were destroyed, and, uniting with Williamson, the two bodies of men swept over the Cherokee valley towns until " all the Cherokee settlements west of the Appalachians had been destroyed from the face of the earth, neither crops nor cattle being left."

While the Carolinians had been sweeping into the lower Cherokee country, the Virginia troops had been assembling at the Long Island of the Holston under their leader Colonel William Christian. Their campaign against the Overhill towns was slowly formed here on the little westward pathway, and it was not until the first of October that all the contributions of men and arms from the settlements between Fort Watauga and the Virginia frontier were received. The advance, by way of Big Island of the Holston, was slow but determined — each encampment being made absolutely secure against surprise. The Indians, learning of the strength of Christian's army, knew better than to resist. They retired without a struggle and the borderers reached the heart of the Overhill country on the fifth day of November. Here they ravaged, burned, and razed to their hearts' content, until a deputation imploring peace came from the broken tribes. In this action old Dragging Canoe would have no part but stole away with a few followers toward the Chickamauga. Christian agreed to a treaty which definitely marked out the boundary line between the Indians and the whites, and then returned home leaving a garrison near the Kentucky path by the Holston. In the words of Roosevelt, who of all writers has done this campaign most justice: " The Watauga people and the westerners generally were the real gainers by the war. Had the Watauga settlements been destroyed, they would no longer have covered the Wilderness Road to Kentucky; and so Kentucky must perforce have been abandoned. But the followers of Robertson and Sevier stood stoutly for their homes; not one of them fled over the mountains. The Cherokees had been so roughly handled that for several years they did not again go to war as a body; and this not only gave the settlers a breathing time, but also enabled them to make themselves so strong that when the struggle was renewed they could easily hold their own. The war was thus another and important link in the chain of events by which the west was won; and had any link in the chain snapped during these early years, the peace of 1783 would probably have seen the trans-Alleghany country in the hands of a non-American power." If the holding of this pathway was of such moment the value of the pathway is plainly understood.

Turning now to the end of Boone's Road, it will be necessary to review briefly the Revolutionary War in the " far " West; though in many of the campaigns the road itself played no part, in a large and genuine sense it was the pilgrims of Boone's Road who fought the most important battles of the Revolution in the West.

Early in the struggle in the West, far-sighted ones saw signs of the growing despicable alliance of the savages to British interests; and before the bloody year of 1778 opened, it was only a question of how much England wanted of the savage allies who were crowded about their forts along the lakes. It is a terrible blot on the history of British rule in America, that when driven to face the same situation, English officers in the West used every means of retaliation for the use of which they so roundly condemned French officials a quarter of a century before. American officers employed Indians as guides and scouts, and were guilty of provoking inter-tribal war; but they did not pay Indians for bringing in British scalps, or praise them for their murderous successes and equip them for further service. As a brave American officer said, " Let this reproach remain on them " — and the people of the West will never forget the reproach, nor forgive! They remember, and always will remember, the burning words of Washington written more than ten years after the close of the Revolution: " All the difficulties we encounter with the Indians, their hostilities, the murder of helpless women and children along all our frontiers, results from the conduct of the agents of Great Britain in this country." There are today, in hundreds of homes of descendants of the pioneers in Kentucky, memories of the inhuman barbarities of British officers during the Revolution; these will never be forgotten, and will never fail to prejudice generations yet unborn. The reproach will remain on them.

At the outbreak of the war, chiefs of the Indian nations were invited to Pittsburg, where the nature of the struggle was explained to them in the following parable:

" Suppose a father had a little son whom he loved and indulged while young, but growing up to be a youth, began to think of having some help from him; and making up a small pack, he bid him carry it for him. The boy cheerfully takes this pack up, following his father with it. The father finding the boy willing and obedient, continues in this way; and as the boy grows stronger, so the father makes the pack in proportion larger; yet as long as the boy is able to carry the pack, he does so without grumbling. At length, however, the boy having arrived at manhood, while the father is making up the pack for him, in comes a person of an evil disposition, and, learning who was to be the carrier of the pack, advises the father to make it heavier, for surely the son is able to carry a larger pack. The father, listening rather to the bad adviser than consulting his own judgment and the feelings of tenderness, follows the advice of the hardhearted adviser, and makes up a heavy load for his son to carry. The son, now grown up, examining the weight of the load he is to carry, addresses the father in these words: ' Dear Father, this pack is too heavy for me to carry, do pray lighten it; I am willing to do what I can, but am unable to carry this load.' The father's heart having by this time become hardened, and the bad adviser calling to him, ' Whip him if he disobeys, ' and he refusing to carry the pack, the father orders his son to take up the pack and carry it off or he will whip him, and already takes up a stick to beat him. ' So,' says the son, ' am I to be served thus for not doing what I am unable to do? Well, if entreaties avail nothing with you, Father, and it is to be decided by blows, whether or not I am able to carry a pack so heavy, then I have no other choice left me, but that of resisting your unreasonable demand by my strength, and thus by striking each other learn who is the strongest.' "

The Indians were urged to become neutral in the struggle that was opening. Impossible as such a course would have been to men who loved war better than peace, certain tribes promised to maintain neutrality. In a few months, however, most of the nations were in open or secret alliance with British officers. Only the better element of the Delaware nation, led by Captain White Eyes, became attached to the American cause. England was always handicapped in her use of the American Indian, because of the want of men who could successfully exert control over him. Even when the forts of the French in the West passed into British possession, Frenchmen were retained in control, since no Englishman could so well rule the savages who made the forts their rendezvous. The beginning of the successful employment of the Indians against the growing Virginian empire south of the Ohio, and against the multiplying cabins and forts of the Long Knives, may loosely be said to have begun in the spring of 1778 when three northern renegades, Simon Girty, Matthew Elliott, and Alexander McKee, eluded the continental General Hand at Pittsburg and took service under Lieutenant-governor Hamilton at Detroit. Bred to border warfare, and well known among the Indians from the Susquehanna to the Missouri, these three men were the " most effective tools for the purposes of border warfare " that the British could have secured. Hamilton immediately began to plan the invasion of Pennsylvania and the conquest of Pittsburg. The campaign was condemned by his superiors in the East, and was forgotten by its originator — when the news of a bold invasion of his own territory by a Virginian army suddenly reached his ears.

The Transylvania Company came silently but suddenly to an end when the Kentuckians elected George Rogers Clark and Gabriel John Jones members of the Virginian assembly, for the assembly erected the county of Kentucky out of the land purchased by Henderson at Fort Watauga in 1775. Upon bringing this about, Clark, a native of Virginia and a hero of Dunmore's War, returned to Kentucky nourishing greater plans. With clear eyes he saw that the increasing affiliation of Indian and British interests meant that England, even though she might be unsuccessful in the East, could keep up an interminable and disastrous warfare " along the rear of the colonies," as long as she held forts on the northern edge of the Black Forest. Clark sent spies northward, who gained information confirming his suspicions; and then he hurried eastward, with his bold plan of conquering the " strongholds of British and Indian barbarity " — Kaskaskia, Vincennes, and Detroit.

He came at a fortunate time. The colonies were rejoicing over the first great victory of the early war, Saratoga. Hope, everywhere, was high. From Patrick Henry, Governor of Virginia, Clark received two orders, one of which was to attack the British post Kaskaskia. He at once set out for Pittsburg to raise, in the West (where both Dunmore and Lewis raised their armies), troops for the most brilliant military achievement in western history. Descending the Ohio to Kentucky, where he received reinforcements, Clark marched silently through the forests — with one hundred and thirty-five chosen men — to Kaskaskia, which he took in utter surprise July 4, 1778. " Keep on with your merriment," he said to revelers whom he surprised at a dance, " but remember you dance under Virginia, not Great Britain." Clark brought the news of the alliance recently made between France and the United States into the Illinois country and used it with telling effect. A French priest at Vincennes raised a Virginian flag over that fort, telling the inhabitants and the Indians that their " French Father had come to life." In October Virginia incorporated the " County of Illinois " within her western empire — the first portion of the land north of the Ohio River to come under the administration of one of the states of the Union.

Contemporaneously with Clark's stirring conquest, an expedition was raised at Pittsburg to march against the Indians in the neighborhood of the British fort at Sandusky — possibly to counteract the rumored attempt to invade Pennsylvania, by Hamilton at Detroit. Troops and supplies were to be assembled at Fort Pitt, where the famous route of Bouquet was to be followed toward the lakes. The expedition was put in charge of General Lachlan Mcintosh. Distressing delays made the half-hearted Indians who were to guide the army, chafe; and Mcintosh started before his stores arrived, fearing that longer delay would alienate his friendly Indians, among whom was the Delaware, White Eyes, now turned from a neutral course. At the mouth of the Beaver River Mcintosh built the fort which bears his name — the first fort built by the Americans on the northern side of the Ohio. Advancing westward over Bouquet's tri-trail track with twelve hundred men, he reached the Muskingum (Tuscarawas) River in fourteen days, arriving November 19, 1778, where he erected Fort Laurens.

But Lieutenant-governor Hamilton, learning of Clark's seizure of Kaskaskia and the treachery of the fickle inhabitants of Vincennes, set about to reconquer Illinois. Departing from Detroit on a beautiful October day, the expedition descended the Detroit River and entered the Maumee. The weather changed and it was seventy-one days before the American Captain Helm at Vincennes surrendered his wretched fort and became a prisoner of war. Hamilton was unable to push on to Kaskaskia because of the lack of provisions, and sat down to watch the winter out where he was. Thus the spectacular year 1778 closed — Clark at Kaskaskia, watching his antagonist feasting at Vincennes; Mcintosh's little guard at Fort Laurens undergoing continual harassing and siege. In the East the evacuation of Philadelphia, the battle of Monmouth, and the terrible Wyoming massacre were the events of the year.

The year 1779 was to see as brilliant an achievement in the West, as the East was to see in the capture of Stony Point. This was the recapture of Vincennes by Clark. Joined by an experienced adventurer, Colonel Francis Vigo, formerly of the Spanish service, Clark was persuaded that he must capture Hamilton or Hamilton would capture him. Accordingly, on the fifth of February, Clark set out for Vincennes with one hundred and seventy trusty men. In twelve days they reached the Embarras River, which was crossed on the twenty-first with great bravery, the men wading in water to their shoulders. On the twenty-fifth, Hamilton, the most surprised man in the world, was compelled to surrender. Within two weeks he was on his way to Virginia; where, being found guilty of buying Virginian scalps from the Indians, he was imprisoned, but was exchanged the year following.

In July, while returning from New Orleans with supplies, Colonel Rogers and his party of Kentuckians were overwhelmed by Indians, under Girty and Elliott, on the Ohio River. In a terrible running battle sixty Kentuckians were killed. The sad news spread quickly through Kentucky and a thousand tongues called loudly for revenge. In response Major Bowman led three hundred volunteers up the Scioto Valley and attacked the Shawanese capital. There was bungling somewhere and a retreat was ordered before victory was achieved.

During this summer the conqueror of Illinois expected to complete his triumph by the capture of Detroit. A messenger from Thomas Jefferson, Governor of Virginia, brought tidings that troops for this expedition would be forthcoming from Virginia and Kentucky, and rendezvous at Vincennes in July. When the time came, Clark found only a few soldiers from Kentucky and none at all from Virginia. The Detroit expedition fell through because of Virginia's poverty in money and in men; though artillery, ammunition, and tools had been secured for the campaign from Fort Pitt, at Washington's command. But with masterly foresight Governor Jefferson secured the establishment of a fort on the Mississippi River in the Illinois country. During this summer the little garrison which General Mcintosh left buried in the Black Forest at Fort Laurens fled back over the trail to Pittsburg. Nowhere north of the Ohio were the scenes frequently enacted in Kentucky reproduced so vividly as at little Fort Laurens, on the upper Muskingum. At one time fourteen of the garrison were decoyed and slaughtered. At another time an army numbering seven hundred warriors invested the little half-forgotten fortress and its intrepid defenders. A slight embankment may be seen today near Bolivar, Ohio, which marks one side of the first fort erected in what is now Ohio, those near the lake shore excepted. Thus closed the year 1779: Clark again in possession of Vincennes, as well as Kaskaskia and Cahokia, but disappointed in the failure of the Detroit expedition; Hamilton languishing in a Virginia dungeon, twelve hundred miles from his capital — Fort Detroit; Fort Laurens abandoned, and the Kentucky country covered with gloom over Rogers's terrible loss and Bowman's inglorious retreat from the valley of the Scioto. On the other hand, the East was glorying in Mad Anthony Wayne's capture of Stony Point, Sullivan's rebuke to the Indians, and Paul Jones's electrifying victory on the sea.

In 1780 four expeditions set forth, all of them singular in character, and noteworthy. The year before, 1779, Spain had declared war upon England. The new commander at Detroit took immediate occasion to regain control of the Mississippi by attacking the Spanish town of St. Louis. This expedition, under Captain Sinclair, descended the Mississippi from Prairie du Chien. The attack was not successful, but six whites were killed and eighteen taken prisoner.

At the time of Bowman's expedition against the Shawanese, in the preceding year a British officer, Colonel Bird, had assembled a noteworthy array at Sandusky preparatory to the invasion of Kentucky. News of the Kentucky raid up the Scioto Valley set Bird's Indians to " cooking and counselling" again, instead of acting. This year Bird's invasion materialized, and the fate of the Kentucky settlements trembled in the balance. The invading army of six hundred Indians and Canadians was armed with two pieces of artillery. There is little doubt that this army could have battered down every " station " in Kentucky and swept victoriously through the new settlements. Ruddles' s station on the Licking was first menaced, and surrendered quickly. Martin's fort also capitulated. But here Bird paused in his conquest and withdrew northward, the barbarity of the Indian allies, for once at least, shocking a British commander. The real secret of the abrupt retreat lay no doubt in the fact that the increasing immigration had brought such vast numbers of people into Kentucky that Bird dared not penetrate further into the land for fear of a surprise. The gross carelessness of the newly arrived inhabitants, in not taking the precaution to build proper defenses against the Indians, undoubtedly appeared to the British commander as a sign of strength and fortitude which he did not have the courage to put to the test. As a matter of fact, he could probably have annihilated every settlement between the Ohio River and Cumberland Gap.

In retaliation Kentucky sent an immense army north of the Ohio, a thousand men volunteering under Clark, the hero of Vincennes. A large Indian army was routed near the Shawanese town Pickaway. Many towns with standing crops were burned. A similar expedition from Pittsburg under General Brodhead burned crops and villages on the upper Muskingum.

In return for the attack on St. Louis, the Spanish commander at that point sent an expedition against the deserted British post of St. Joseph. Upon declaring war against England in the previous year, Spain had occupied Natchez, Baton Rouge, and Mobile, which, with St. Louis, gave her command of the Mississippi. But his Catholic Majesty was building other Spanish castles in America. He desired the conquest of the British northwest, to offset the

British capture of Gibraltar. This " capture " of St. Joseph led to an amusing but ominous claim on the part of Spain at the Treaty of Paris: when, with it for a pretext, the Spanish Crown claimed all lands west of a line drawn from St. Joseph southward through what is now Ohio, Kentucky, Tennessee, Georgia, Alabama, and Mississippi. The Mississippi River boundary was, however, stoutly contended for and obtained by the American commissioners.

In this year the first " gunboat" to ply western waters was built under direction of Brigadier-general Clark. It was a galley armed with light artillery. This queer-looking craft soon fell into disuse, though it became a terror to the Indians who continually infested the lower Ohio. It was relished little better by the militia, who disliked service on water. But it stands as a typical illustration of the enterprise and devotion of the " Father of Kentucky" to the cause for which he had done so much.

The year following, 1781, saw the termination of the Revolution in the East, when Cornwallis's army marched down the files of French and American troops at Yorktown to the melancholy tune " The World's Turned Upside Down." The Treaty of Paris was not signed until 1783, and in the meantime the bloodiest year of all the war in the West, 1782, was adding its horrors to all that had gone before. While the East was rejoicing, the central West saw the terrible massacre of Gnadenhutten — the more terrible because committed by white men themselves.

In May, 1782, the atrocities of the savages (encouraged by the British) along the Pennsylvanian and Virginian border were becoming unbearable, and an expedition was raised in the Monongahela country to penetrate to the Indian-infested country on the Sandusky River. Volunteers, four hundred in number, all mounted, rendezvoused at the Ohio near Mingo Bottom; they elected as commander Colonel William Crawford, an experienced officer of the Revolutionary War, following Washington faithfully through the hard Long Island and Delaware campaigns. Crawford struck straight through the forests, even avoiding Indian trails, at first, in the hope of taking his foe utterly by surprise. But his wily foe completely outwitted him and the Indians and British knew well each day's progress. The battle was fought in a prairie land near the Sandusky River in what is now Crawford County, Ohio, and though not a victory for either side, an American retreat was ordered during the night following. Colonel Crawford was captured, among others, and suffered a terrible death at the stake, perhaps the saddest single atrocity committed by the red man in western history. This gray-haired veteran of the Revolution gave his life to appease the Indians for a massacre of Christian Indians perpetrated by savage borderers from the Monongahela country the year previous.

Kentucky had witnessed minor activities of the savages during the spring. In August a grand Indian army assembled on the lower Scioto for the purpose of invading Kentucky. The assembly was harangued by Simon Girty, and moved southward and invaded Bryant's Station, one of the strongest forts in Kentucky.

After a terrible day, during which reinforcements kept arriving, only to be compelled to fight their way into the fort or flee, Girty attempted to secure capitulation. Outwitted, the renegade resorted to a stratagem, as cunningly devised as it was terribly successful. In the night the entire Indian army vanished as if panic-stricken. Meat was left upon the spits. Garments lay strewn about the encampment and along the route of the fugitive army. The more experienced of the border army, which was soon in full cry on the trail, scented the deception; but the headstrong hurried onward in hope of revenge. At the crossing of the Licking, near the lower Blue Licks, the Indian ambush received the witless pursuers with a frightful burst of flame, and the battle of Blue Licks became a running fire, a headlong rout and massacre.

A thousand men joined Clark for a retaliatory invasion of the north, and the usual destruction of villages and crops was accomplished. This may be considered the last military event in the Revolutionary War in the West.

CHAPTER V - AT THE END OF BOONE'S ROAD

ON the nineteenth of April, 1775, the rumble of the running fire at Lexington and Concord told that the farmers of New England had at last precipitated the struggle which had been impending for a full generation. It was a roar that, truly, was " heard round the world." One day later, April 20, 1775, Colonel Henderson and his fellow-pioneers of the Transylvania Company reached Boonesborough; there they were joyfully received by a running fire of five and twenty muskets discharged by Boone's vanguard, which had preceded them to cut the road. If the musket-shot behind the New England stone walls was heard round the world, the rattle of that score of muskets in distant Kentucky was heard around a continent. The former uttered a hoarse defiance to tyrants — a cry to God for liberty; what was the faint roar which echoed back a thousand mountain miles from Kentucky but an answer to that cry? an assurance that " to him that hath shall be given? " There is something divinely significant to me in the coincidence of the opening shock of the Revolution, and the arrival in Kentucky of the first considerable body of determined, reputable men.

The story of the Revolutionary War in the West has been told in preceding pages, as the merest record of fact. It is unnecessary to state that it was the most important conflict ever waged there, and it is equally trite to observe that the struggle centered around Kentucky. Boone's Road had made possible the sudden movement of population westward, and this pioneer host immediately drew upon itself the enemies that otherwise would have scourged the frontiers of New York, Pennsylvania, Virginia, and North Carolina. The first and principal portion of the Kentucky pioneers — those who fought the Revolutionary battles — entered Kentucky by the Cumberland Gap route. James Lane Allen writes: " That area [Kentucky] has somewhat the shape of an enormous flat foot, with a disjointed big toe, a roughly hacked-off ankle, and a missing heel. The sole of this huge foot rests solidly on Tennessee, the Ohio River trickles across the ankle and over the top, the big toe is washed entirely off by the Tennessee River, and the long-missing heel is to be found in Virginia, never having been ceded by that State. Between the Kentucky foot and the Virginia heel is piled up this immense, bony, grisly mass of the Cumberland Mountain, extending some three hundred miles northeast and southwest. It was through this heel that Kentucky had to be peopled. The thin, half-starved, weary line of pioneer civilizers had to penetrate it, and climb this obstructing mountain wall, as a line of traveling ants might climb the wall of a castle. In this case only the strongest of the ants — the strongest in body, the strongest in will — succeeded in getting over and establishing their colony in the country far beyond. Luckily there was an enormous depression in the wall, or they might never have scaled it. During about half a century this depression was the difficult, exhausting entrance-point through which the State received the largest part of its people, the furniture of their homes, and the implements of their civilization; so that from the very outset that people represented the most striking instance of a survival of the fittest that may be observed in the founding of any American commonwealth. The feeblest of the ants could not climb the wall; the idlest of them would not." Mr. Speed agrees wholly in this opinion: " The settlers came in . . increasing numbers. . . A very large proportion came over the Wilderness Road." In the early days river travel was not practicable. During the Revolutionary War and for some time thereafter travel down the Ohio River was dangerous, both because of the hostility of the savages and because of the condition of the river. In earlier days the journey from the Ohio into the populated parts of Kentucky was a great hardship. The story of one who emigrated to Kentucky by way of the Ohio shows plainly why many preferred the longer land route by way of Cumberland Gap. The following is from an autobiographical statement made by Spencer Record, preserved by the Wisconsin Historical Society:

" About the Twentieth of November (1783) we embarked on the Monongahela in our boat, in company with Kiser, I having with me four head of horses and some cattle. We landed at the mouth of Limestone Creek, but there was then, no settlement there. We made search for a road, but found none. There was indeed a buffalo road, that crossed Limestone Creek a few miles above its mouth, and passing May's lick about twelve miles from Limestone, went on to the Lower Blue Lick on Licking river, and thence to Bryant's station: but as we knew nothing of it, we went on, and landed at the mouth of Licking river, on the twenty ninth of the month.

" The next day, we loaded periogue, and a canoe, and set off up Licking, sometimes wading and pulling our periogue and canoe over the ripples. After working hard for four days, we landed, hid our property (which was whiskey and our farming utensils) in the woods, and returned to the Ohio, which by this time had taken a rapid rise and backed up Licking, so that we took Riser's boat up, as far as we had taken our property and unloaded her. We left on the bank of Licking, a new wagon and some kettles. Leaving our property to help Kiser, we packed up and set off up Licking, and travelled some days; but making poor progress, and snow beginning to fall, with no cane in that part of the country, for our horses and cattle, we left Kiser and set off to hunt for cane. He sent his stock with us, in care of Henry Fry, who had come down in his boat with cattle for his father.

" When we came to the fork of Licking we found a wagon road cut out, that led up the South fork. This road had been cut by Colonel Bird, a British officer, who had ascended Licking in keel boats, with six hundred Canadians and Indians. They were several days in cutting out this road which led to Riddle's fort, which stood on the east side of Licking, three miles below the junction of Hinkston's and Stoner's fork, yet our people knew nothing of it, till they were summoned to surrender. . . We took the road and went on, the snow being about half leg deep. Early in the morning, about three miles from Riddle's fort, we came to three families encamped. They had landed at Limestone but finding no road, they wandered through the woods, crossed Licking, and happening to find the road, took it. . . We went on to the fort, where we found plenty of cane. The next morning, John Finch and myself set off to try to find Lexington, and left the horses and cattle. . . as there was no road, we took up Will creek, and towards the head of it we met some hunters, who lived on the south side of Kentucky river who gave us directions how to find a hunting trace, that led to Bryant's station. . . We went on, found the trace, and arrived at Bryant's station."

Adding to the difficulties of land travel the dangers of the river tide, the difficulty of securing boats, and their great cost, it is little wonder that emigrants from Virginia preferred the long but better-known land route, through Powell's Valley and Cumberland Gap to the Braddock Road and the Ohio River. At a later date, however, the difficulties of river passage were materially decreased and the Ohio became the great outward emigrant route.

But for the return traffic from Kentucky to Virginia, there was no comparison between the ease of the land route and the water route. Mr. Speed affirms that the road through Cumberland Gap " was the only practicable route for all return travel." Of course for a long period there were no exports from Kentucky, as hardly enough could be raised to feed the multitude of immigrants; but when at last Kentucky strode to the front with its great harvests of wheat and tobacco, the Mississippi and Ohio ports received them.

The East received comparatively little benefit, in a commercial way, from Boone's Road; but in the earliest days that slight track furnished a moral support that can hardly be exaggerated. The vast population that surged westward over it was a mighty barrier which protected the rear of the colonies from the savages, until savage warfare was at an end. Though the frontiers of New York, Pennsylvania, and Virginia suffered greatly during the Revolution, it was Kentucky that was the thorn in the side of the British; Kentucky drew the fire of both British and Indians which otherwise would have desolated the rear of the eastern colonies, and necessitated a greater number of men than could possibly have been maintained there. It was not at Fort Pitt that the British were constantly striking, but at the Kentucky " stations; " it was not up the Allegheny or Monongahela that Colonel Burd pushed his keel boats, but up the Licking. This fact is splendidly urged by Col. John Floyd, in a letter to the governor of Virginia written on the sixth of October, 1781, in a plea for assistance in maintaining the Kentucky settlements:

" . . A great deal more might be said concerning the dangerous situation of these counties, but I have not been informed whether Government think it absolutely necessary for the advantage of the community at large to defend this country [Kentucky] at so considerable expense as must be incurred thereby; and I therefore beg leave to offer your Excellency one or two reasons why it may be of advantage to defend the Kentucky country. It is now beyond a doubt, that the attention of at last [least] 6000 savage warriors is fixed on this spot, and who will not disturb any other part of the Continent as long as we maintain our ground. But, on the contrary, as soon as this country is laid waste, they will immediately fall upon the inhabitants of Washington, Montgomery, Greenbriar, &c — in short, from South Carolina to Pennsylvania. I believe all the counties on the west side of the Blue Ridge were kept for many years penned up in forts by the Shawanese, Mingoes, Delawares & a few of their adherents; if so what will be the consequence when at least fifteen powerful Nations are united and combined with those above mentioned against about twelve hundred militia dispersed over three very extensive counties. Those nations have absolutely been kept off your back settlements by the inhabitants of Kentucky. Two or three thousand men in this country would be sufficient to defend it, and effectually secure the back settlements on New River & its waters, as well as those high up James River & Roanoake "

In addition to conferring the inestimable advantage of defending the frontiers of the colonies, the early settlement and the holding of Kentucky insured American possession of the Middle West; this meant everything to the East — for the steady, logical expansion of the nation was the one hope of the country when independence was secured. Upon the Americanization of the Mississippi Valley depended the safety of the eastern colonies, and their commercial and political welfare. It meant very much to the East that a strong colony was holding its own on the Ohio and Mississippi during the hours when the Revolutionary struggle was in progress; and it meant even more to the East that, upon the conclusion of that struggle, thousands whose future seemed as black as the forests of the West could immediately emigrate thither and begin life anew. But for the Virginians and Kentuckians along the Ohio it is almost certain that Great Britain would have divided the eastern half of this continent with the triumphant revolutionists. For the few posts along the lakes that she did hold there was a spirited wrangle for twenty years, until they were at last handed over to the United States. Boone did not blaze his road one day too soon, and the hand of divine Providence is not shown more plainly in our national history than by the critical timeliness with which these pioneers were ushered into the meadow lands of Ken-ta-kee. The onslaughts of Shawanese and Wyandot did not overwhelm them; nor were they daunted by the plotting of desperate British officers, who spread ruin and desolation along the flank and rear of the fighting colonies.

Again, this earliest population in the immediate valley of the Mississippi had a powerful influence on the attitude of the United States toward the powers that held the Mississippi. Had it not been for a Kentucky in embryo in 1775-82, it is unquestionable that the confused story of the possession of that great river valley would have been worse confounded. The whirl of politics in Kentucky during the four decades after the Revolutionary War daunts even the student of modern Kentucky politics; and of one thing we may rest assured — had the State possessed a little less of the sober sense that came from Virginia through Cumberland Gap, it is certain the story of those wild days would not be as readable to modern Kentuckians as it is. It was more than fortunate for the young Republic that at the close of the Revolution there was a goodly population of expatriated Virginians and North Carolinians on the Mississippi, ready to press its claims there.

Thus we may briefly suggest the benefits which the older colonies received from the earliest settlers in Kentucky — and but for Boone's Road made by the Transylvania Company, it is exceedingly doubtful, as Boone wrote, whether the settlement of Kentucky would have been successfully inaugurated as early as 1774. At any rate Boone's Road brought into Kentucky thousands of pioneers who probably would have refused to move westward by the Ohio River route.

As for the benefit Kentucky itself received from Boone's Road, that is self-evident. Taking everything into consideration, no distinct movement of population in America, before or since, can compare in magnitude with the burst of immigration through Cumberland Gap between 1775 and 1790. Never on this continent was a population of seventy thousand people located, within fifteen years of the day the first cabins were erected, at an equal distance from the existing frontier line. It is difficult to frame the facts of this remarkable phenomenon in language that will convey the full meaning. If the brave pioneers from Connecticut who founded the Northwest Territory at Marietta, Ohio, in 1788, had gone on to Kentucky, they would have found themselves, within twelve years, in as populous a state as that they left in New England. The Stanwix Treaty and Boone's Road largely answer the question why Kentucky contained more than one-half as many inhabitants as Massachusetts, twenty-five years after its first settlement was made; and why it was admitted into the Union four years before Tennessee, ten years before Ohio, twenty-four years before Indiana, twenty-six years before Illinois (bounded by the Ohio and Mississippi and Lake Michigan), and twenty-eight years before Maine. Between 1790 and 1800 the population of Kentucky jumped from 70,000 to 220,000, only one-third less than proud Maryland, and five times that of Ohio. In the census of 1790 Kentucky stood fourteenth in a grouping of sixteen states and territories, while in 1800 it stood ninth. In 1790 it exceeded the population of Rhode Island, Delaware and Tennessee. In 1800 it exceeded New Jersey, New Hampshire, Georgia, Vermont, Maine, Tennessee, Rhode Island, and Delaware. In this year it had one hundred and sixty thousand more inhabitants than Indiana Territory, Mississippi Territory, and Ohio Territory combined. In the decade mentioned, New York State increased in population two hundred and fifty thousand; far-away Kentucky increased one hundred and forty-seven thousand.

But the West as a whole was benefited by Boone's Road. The part played by this earliest population of Kentucky in the development of the contiguous states — Ohio, Indiana, Illinois, and Missouri — has never been emphasized sufficiently. No Ohio historian has given sufficient attention to the part played by Kentuckians in the conquest of that area of territory. The struggle between the Kentuckians and the Ohio Indians has been outlined. The former fought for and saved to the Union the great territory south of the Ohio; and then left their smoking cabins and threw themselves ever and anon across the Ohio, upon the Indian settlements between that river and the Great Lakes. Where is even the Kentucky historian who has done his state justice in telling the story of Kentucky's conquest of Ohio and Indiana? Of the brilliant operations of Clark in Illinois we know very much, and the part played by the Kentuckians on the Mississippi and Illinois has frequently been made plain. But a singular misconception of the nature of Indian warfare has robbed the heroes of old Kentucky of much honor due them. Judged by ordinary military standards, the numerous invasions of Ohio and Indiana by Kentuckians amounted to little. Such was not the real case, many times. The Indians could ever retreat helter-skelter into the forests, avoiding more than a mere skirmish with the advancing pioneers. But they could not take their crops — and the destruction of one slight maize crop meant more to the invading army than the killing of many savages. The killing of the Indians did nothing but aggravate hostilities and long delay the end of the conflict. On the other hand, slaying redskins became the passion of the whites, and it is probable that many of their expeditions seemed failures if blood was not spilt. But their very presence in the Indian land and the destruction of the grain fields was more to their purpose, could they only have realized it. The Indians were then compelled to live largely on game, and as this grew more scarce each year the simple problem of obtaining subsistence became serious. The hunters were compelled to go further and further into the forest, and the tribes followed them. By doing nothing more than burning the harvest fields and ruining the important springs, the whites were slowly but surely conquering the trans-Ohio country. By such a process one river valley after another was deserted, until, when the first legalized settlement was made in Ohio — at Marietta, in 1788 — the Muskingum, Scioto and Miami valleys were practically deserted by redskins. Little as the Indians relished the new settlement at Marietta, they paid practically no attention to it but kept their eyes on the populated valleys of Kentucky, where their enemies of so many years' standing had settled, held their own, and then carried fire and sword northward. In October 1788 Governor Arthur St. Clair wrote the Hon. Mr. Brown of Danville, Kentucky, to give warning of the Indian war that seemed imminent; " The stroke, if it falls at all, will probably fall upon your country," he wrote. And the Indian War of 1790 was precipitated because of Indian marauds along the Kentucky border — not because of attacks upon the settlements along the upper Ohio. The Kentuckians had played a preeminent part in driving the Indians back to the head of the Wabash and the mouth of the Maumee, in the two decades preceding the Indian War which opened in 1790, and during that war they were to the American armies what the English were to the allies at Waterloo. Local histories and local historians have created the impression that Ohio was conquered largely by Ohioans. Nothing could be more misleading.

Far-reaching as the influence of the little roadway through Cumberland Gap has been, its actual history is of little interest or importance. Perhaps none of our ancient roads has done so much for society in proportion to the attention paid to it. Any adjective ever applied to a roadway, if it were of a derogatory character, might have been fitly applied to portions of this old track which played an important part in giving birth to the first and most important settlement in the West. During the few important years of its existence Boone's Road was only what Boone made it — a blazed foot-path westward. It was but the merest foot-path from 1774 to 1792, while thousands floundered over its uncertain track to lay the rude foundations of civilization in the land to which it led. " There are roads that make a man lose faith," writes Mr. Allen; "It is known that the more pious companies [of pioneers] as they traveled along, would now and then give up in despair, sit down, raise a hymn, and have prayers said before they could go farther. " There was probably not a more desperate pioneer road in America than this. The mountains to be crossed, the rivers and swamps the traveler encountered, were as difficult to overcome as any on Braddock's Road; and Boone's Road was very much longer, even if measured from its technical starting-point — the Watauga settlement.

As early as 1779 the Virginia Assembly took up the subject of a western highway, and commissioners were appointed to explore the region on both sides of the mountains, to choose a course for a roadway, clear and open the route, and render a report upon the advisability of making a wagon road. Yet no improvement followed. The narrow path — rough, treacherous, almost impassable — remained the only course. A vivid description of what a journey over it meant in this year, 1779, has been left us by Chief-justice Robertson in an address given at Camp Madison, Franklin County, Kentucky, half a century ago:

" This beneficent enactment [the land law] brought to the country during the fall and winter of that year an unexampled tide of emigrants, who, exchanging all the comforts of their native society and homes for settlements for themselves and their children here, came like pilgrims to a wilderness to be made secure by their arms and habitable by the toil of their lives. Through privations incredible and perils thick, thousands of men, women, and children came in successive caravans, forming continuous streams of human beings, horses, cattle, and other domestic animals, all moving onward along a lonely and houseless path to a wild and cheerless land. Cast your eyes back on that long procession of missionaries in the cause of civilization; behold the men on foot with their trusty guns on their shoulders, driving stock and leading packhorses; and the women, some walking with pails on their heads, others riding with children in their laps, and other children swung in baskets on horses, fastened to the tails of others going before; see them encamped at night expecting to be massacred by Indians; behold them in the month of December, in that ever memorable season of unprecedented cold called the 'hard winter,' traveling two or three miles a day, frequently in danger of being frozen or killed by the falling of horses on the icy and almost impassable trace, and subsisting on stinted allowances of stale bread and meat; but now lastly look at them at the destined fort, perhaps on the eve of merry Christmas, when met by the hearty welcome of friends who had come before, and cheered by fresh buffalo meat and parched corn, they rejoice at their deliverance, and resolve to be contented with their lot.

" This is no vision of the imagination, it is but an imperfect description of the pilgrimage of my own father and mother, and of many others who settled in Kentucky in December, 1779."

Not until 1792 was the mountain route improved. " In that year," writes Mr. Speed, " according to an account-book recently found among the Henry Innis Papers, by Colonel John Mason Brown . a scheme was projected for the clearing and improvement of the Wilderness Road, under the direction of Colonel John Logan and James Knox. It was a private enterprise altogether; the subscribers to it are set down in the book.

" Besides these, it appears from a note in the memorandum book there were other subscribers. Among the Innis papers I have found the following paper:

' Colonel John Logan and Colonel James Knox, having consented to act as commissioners to direct and supervise the making and opening a road from the Crab Orchard to Powell's Valley, provided funds to defray the necessary expenses shall be procured, we, the subscribers, do therefore severally engage to pay the sum annexed to our names to the Hon. Harry Innis and Colonel Levi Todd, or to their order, in trust, to be by them applied to the payment of the reasonable expenses which the said commissioners may incur in carrying the above design into effect, also to the payment of such compensation to the said commissioners for their services as the said Innis and Todd may deem adequate.'

June 20, 1792.
Thos. Barber, $10
Wm. Crow, 5
Green Dorsey, 18

John Cochran, 4
David Gillis, 10
Wm. Petty, 1
John Warren, 10
Wm. Kenton, 1
Philip Bush, jr., 10
David Rice, 1
John Rochester, 10
John Rogers, 1
Samuel G. Keen, 5
Padtrick Curran, 1
John Reedyun, 1
Daniel Barber, 1
Philip Yeiser, 3

" The money subscribed was disbursed by Harry Innis. Men were employed as ' road cutters, ' as ' surveyors, ' to ' carry provisions,' to ' grind corn,' and ' collect bacon.' The pay was two shillings sixpence per day, and the work extended over twenty-two days in the summer of 1792." The Kentucky legislature passed an act in 1793, which provided a guard for pilgrims on the Wilderness Road; in 1794 an act was passed for the clearing of the Boonesborough fork of the road, from Rockcastle Creek to the Kentucky River. In 1795 the legislature passed an act to make the Wilderness Road a "wagon road" thirty feet wide from near Crab Orchard to Cumberland Gap. Proposals being advertised for, the aged Daniel Boone addressed Governor Isaac Shelby the following letter:

" Sir feburey the 11th 1796

after my Best Respts to your Excelancy and famyly I wish to inform you that I have sum intention of undertaking this New Rode that is to be Cut through the Wilderness and I think My Self intiteled to the ofer of the Bisness as I first Marked out that Rode in March 1775 and Never Re'd anything for my trubel and Sepose I am No Statesman I am a Woodsman and think My Self as Capable of Marking and Cutting that Rode as any other man Sir if you think with Me I would thank you to wright mee a Line by the post the first oportuneaty and he Will Lodge it at Mr. John Miler son hinkston fork as I wish to know Where and When it is to be Laat [let] So that I may atend at the time

I am Deer Sir your very omble sarvent "

Boone probably did not get the contract. In 1797 five hundred pounds were appropriated for the repair of the road and erection of toll-gates. The result of this and all subsequent legislation, to preserve a thoroughfare after its day and reason for existence had passed, is thus summed up by Mr. Allen: " But despite all this — despite all that has been done to civilize it since Boone traced its course in 1790 [1775?], this honored historic thoroughfare remains today as it was in the beginning, with all its sloughs and sands, its mud and holes, and jutting ledges of rock and loose boulders, and twists and turns, and general total depravity." And yet "it is impossible," Mr. Allen continues, " to come upon this road without pausing, or to write of it without a tribute."

The mountainous portions of Boone's old road are the picturesque as well as the historic portions. And come what may, this zig-zag pathway through Powell's Valley and Cumberland Gap can never be effaced — never forgotten. The footsteps of the tens of thousands who have passed over it, exhausted though each pilgrim may have been, have left a trace that a thousand years cannot eradicate. And so long as the print of those weary feet can be seen in dark Powell's Valley, on Cumberland Gap, and beside Yellow and Rockcastle Creeks, so long will there be a memorial left to perpetuate the heroism of the first Kentuckians— and the memory of what the Middle West owes to Virginia and her neighbors. For when all is said this track from tide water through Cumberland Gap must remain a monument to the courage and patriotism of the people of old Virginia and North Carolina.

Cumberland Gap, " that high-swung gateway through the mountain" stands as " a landmark of what Nature can do when she wishes to give an opportunity to the human race in its migrations and discoveries, without surrendering control of its liberty and its fate." Here passed the mound-building Indian and the buffalo, marking the first routes from North to South across the continent. Here later passed the first flood-tide of white men's immigration. There are few spots on the continent, it is said, where the traveler of today is brought more quickly to a pause, overcome equally by the stupendous panorama before him, and by the memory of the historical associations which will assail even the most indifferent. Ere you reach the Gap " the idea of it," writes Mr. Allen, " dominates the mind. While yet some miles away, it looms up, 1675 feet in elevation, some half a mile across from crest to crest, the pinnacle on the left towering to the height of 2500 feet. It was late in the afternoon when our tired horses began the long, winding, rocky climb from the valley to the brow of the pass. As we stood in the passway, amid the deepening shadows of the twilight and the solemn repose of the mighty landscape, the Gap seemed to be crowded with two invisible and countless pageants of human life, the one passing in, the other passing out; and the air grew thick with unheard utterances — primeval sounds undistinguishable and strange, of creatures nameless and never seen by man; the wild rush and whoop of retreating and pursuing tribes; the slow steps of watchful pioneers; the wail of dying children and the songs of homeless women; the muffled tread of routed and broken armies — all the sounds of surprise and delight, victory and defeat, hunger and pain, and weariness and despair, that the human heart can utter. Here passed the first of the white race who led the way into the valley of the Cumberland; here passed that small band of fearless men who gave the Gap its name; here passed the '

Long Hunters '; here rushed armies of the Civil War; here has passed the wave of westerly immigration, whose force has spent itself only on the Pacific slopes; and here in the long future must flow backward and forward the wealth of the North and the South."

www.ingramcontent.com/pod-product-compliance
Lightning Source LLC
Chambersburg PA
CBHW071930020426
42331CB00010B/2799